PYREX®

THE UNAUTHORIZED COLLECTOR'S GUIDE

REVISED
&
EXPANDED
3RD EDITION

BARBARA MAUZY

Schiffer Publishing Ltd®

4880 Lower Valley Road, Atglen, PA 19310 USA

DEDICATION

This book is dedicated to my husband and best friend, Jim. I originally started working on this several years ago and he supported me and tolerated me and continued to love me through all of the trials and tribulations and time away from home. I will always love you, Barbara.

This book is also dedicated to our most special friend, partner, co-conspirator, "adopted child" and invaluable helper, David G. Baker. We met over Peanut Butter Glasses and have become the deepest and truest of friends since! -Barbara E. Mauzy

This book is also dedicated to Timothy Brubaker for his long-suffering tolerance of my PYREX® passion. Thanks! -David Mitchell

A NOTE FROM BARBARA: If you enjoy collecting PYREX® Jim and I recommend you shop at 272 Antiques and Collectibles 1300 North Reading Road, Stevens, PA. (717.336.0888) We buy and sell at this wonderful market found just three miles south of Exit 21/286 of the Pennsylvania Turnpike on Route 272. Open seven days a week, you will find great merchandise including PYREX®. And don't forget our website: www.TPTT.net.

Revised price guide: 2004
Copyright © 2000, 2002 & 2004 by Barbara E. Mauzy
Library of Congress Control Number: 2003113586

Book Design by Anne Davidsen
Cover Design by Bruce Waters
Type set in LithographLight /Zapf Humanist

ISBN: 0-7643-1907-8
Printed in China
1 2 3 4

Published by Schiffer Publishing Ltd.
4880 Lower Valley Road
Atglen, PA 19310
Phone: (610) 593-1777; Fax: (610) 593-2002
E-mail: Info@schifferbooks.com
Please visit our web site catalog at **www.schifferbooks.com**
We are always looking for people to write books on new and related subjects. If you have an idea for a book please contact us at the above address.

This book may be purchased from the publisher.
Include $3.95 for shipping.
Please try your bookstore first.
You may write for a free catalog.

In Europe, Schiffer books are distributed by
Bushwood Books
6 Marksbury Ave.
Kew Gardens
Surrey TW9 4JF England
Phone: 44 (0) 20 8392-8585; Fax: 44 (0) 20 8392-9876
E-mail: info@bushwoodbooks.co.uk
Free postage in the U.K., Europe; air mail at cost.

CONTENTS

ABOUT THE PRICES

Everything possible has been done to provide accurate prices. The author has monitored the Internet, auctions, and trade papers, gone to shows, and consulted with collectors and dealers alike. Also brought to this effort are years of experience, personally buying, selling, and collecting glassware.

This book is designed to be a tool and a reference for identification, and—hopefully—a treasured part of your personal library. Values vary immensely according to the condition of the piece, the location of the market, and the overall quality of the design and manufacture. Condition is always of paramount importance when assigning a value. The prices shown in this reference are for individual items that are in mint condition, sometimes with the original package. Prices throughout the country differ greatly, and prices at shows are sometimes higher than those at a shop or flea market. And, of course, being at the right place at the right time can make all the difference.

All of these factors make it impossible to create an absolutely accurate pricing structure, but this reference will offer a guide. The values shown in this book reflect what one could realistically expect to pay.

Neither the author nor the publisher are responsible for any outcomes resulting from consulting this reference.

ACKNOWLEDGMENTS

There were many people whose tireless efforts behind the scenes at Schiffer Publishing allowed this project to easily come together. First of all, thanks go to Jerry Fronefield and Ernie Barrett who sorted, wrapped, and carried PYREX® for hours on end! (Hand! Machine!) Thanks, guys! My thanks are also extended to Tammy Ward and Robyn Stoltzfus for unwrapping, sorting, washing, wrapping, unwrapping, sorting, and once again rewrapping PYREX®. I don't think these burdensome chores were part of their job descriptions, but they labored pleasantly, making my job unbelievably easier! Thanks to Molly Higgins my photographer and now friend, who brought new meaning to the words "confrontational glass!" Thanks to Bruce Waters, a great designer and special friend, who provided another absolutely fantastic cover!

INTRODUCTION

Amory Houghton, Sr. began his career in the wharf business but left that to establish the Union Glass Company in Somerville, Massachusetts, in 1851. This business was sold in 1864; but, in the same year, Amory purchased the Brooklyn Flint Glass Company in Brooklyn, New York. Four years later, this plant and one hundred employees moved by canal boat to Corning, New York, and the renamed business became Corning Flint Glass Works.

Initially, this new factory focused upon tablewares, thermometer tubing, and conventional glasswares. But, in an era of steep competition and with a large debt structure, Amory Houghton was forced to sell his control of the operation in 1871.

Amory's son, Amory Houghton, Jr., was both a chemist and businessman. He worked his way up the corporate ladder and became a manager. His motivation and savvy paid off and Amory Houghton, Jr. soon bought control of the facility.

In 1875, Corning Glass Works became incorporated. Amory Houghton, Jr. was the first president, with his brother, Charles F., just under him. The products manufactured were predominately railroad signal glassware, thermometer tubing and pharmaceutical glassware. The first light bulb blanks were produced for Thomas Edison at the plant in 1879. This proved to be a very positive relationship for Corning Glass Works.

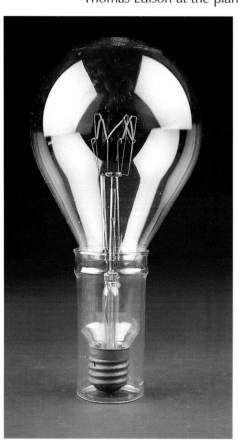

Amory Houghton, Jr.'s health began to deteriorate in 1889, and his son, Alanson, joined the family business as shipping clerk with a wage of $1.25 per day. Alanson, who later became known as "A.B.", began the task of learning all aspects of the business and eventually oversaw sales while his father remained president.

Alanson's brother, Arthur, who became known as "A.A.", acquired control of production. It was Arthur's development of machinery capable of the vertical drawing of thermometer tubing in 1897 that propelled the company into more profitable endeavors and greater success followed.

Automatic incandescent bulb-blowing machines were developed in 1907. The Railroad Signal Association accepted Corning Glass Works signal glassware colors as the standard for all American and Canadian railways in 1908. This was particularly important for the safety of those using railways. Now red signals were truly red, not shades of amber or yellow, and green was green, not one of 32 shades of green. These past variations may have contributed to loss of life when an engineer misread a signal.

This light bulb was made by Corning Glass Works, c. 1880.

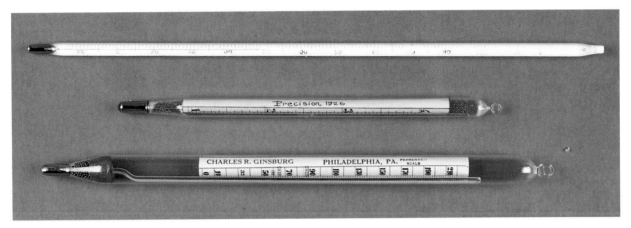

Three thermometers made with Corning glass. *Top:* 12" long; *middle:* 8" long and marked "Precision 1926;" *bottom:* 10.25" long and marked: "Charles R. Ginsberg Philadelphia PA."

Dr. Eugene C. Sullivan's Corning Glass Works research laboratory developed glassware with new and improved properties. First, his research led to the creation of heat-resistant glass to be used in railroad lanterns. Hand held lanterns were often used to signal a passenger train, particularly at night. Prior to this development, hot lantern globes were susceptible to breakage in cold weather. Battery jars were also developed at this time. These containers protected humans from the dangerous chemicals used in batteries.

A 14.5" glass container to store a car battery marked: "PYREX® TE REG US PAT OFF MADE IN USA 50006."

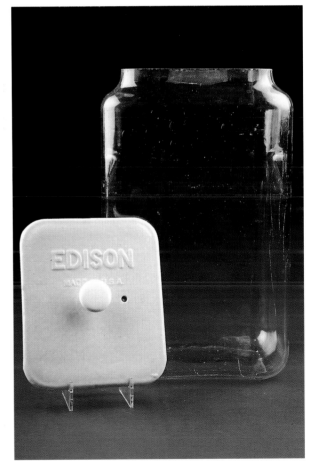

Note the Edison name on the lid of this battery box.

The tenth anniversary of PYREX® kitchen glass is recognized and celebrated in an advertisement offering lower prices.

An early example of PYREX® glass utilized for scientific purposes.

Amory Houghton, Jr. passed away in 1910 and "A.B." became the next president of Corning Glass Works. He retained this position until 1918. Many important developments occurred during his tenure.

PYREX® brand glassware was introduced in 1915. This new glassware had incredible resistence to thermal expansion and contraction, making it very tolerant of sudden and extreme temperature changes. Its roots were in the heat resistant glass developed for railroad use.

PYREX® brand chemical ware, introduced in 1917, was inpervious to chemicals. This high level of resistance allowed scientists and researchers to conduct their work knowing the results would not be tainted. Chemicals in the glass itself would not be co-mingling with those researchers were placing inside the glass.

Control of the Corning Glass Works stayed within the Houghton family, whose vision, intelligence, and management skills resulted in a company that stayed on the forefront of research and development.

Corning Glass Works had a relationship with a number of its competitors. From 1918-1921, J. Hoare & Company created engravings on PYREX® glassware in an agreement with Corning Glass Works. In 1920, Fry Glass Company was granted a licence to produce PYREX® with the name "Fry Oven Glass." McKee Glass Company established an agreement with Corning Glass Works in 1921 that later was renewed to include FLAMEWARE. Macbeth-Evans Glass Company merged with Corning Glass Works in 1936, and in 1937 Pittsburgh-Corning Corporation was created to manufacture glass blocks. As you look at PYREX® throughout this book, you will also see examples of kitchen glass with PYREX® parts and another company's name.

Major innovations in glass production continued, including the development of the glass Ribbon Machine and the 200-inch disk which became the Mt. Palomar telescopic mirror. Begun in 1931, completed in 1936, and weighing over twenty tons, it was the largest piece of glass ever cast. Manufacturing of glass fibers started in 1939, the first automated production of optical glass occurred in 1944, and the first automated production of television tubes and photosensitive glass were both introduced in 1947.

Corning Glass Works products have become a part of business, industry, homes, and schools. PYREX® is but a small part of the Corning Glass Works story of a highly successful, family-run organization. From Ovenware to FLAMEWARE to PYREX® colors, this book will focus on PYREX® glassware in the American home.

Loaf pan measuring 5" x 10" with engraving.

A 1916 advertisement for Fry's Oven Glass.

June 1922 advertisement for Fry's Oven Glass.

October 1922 advertisement for Fry's Oven Glass.

Fry Oven Glass Bakers, two with lids. *Left to right:* 2.75"deep x 8.5", 2" deep x 7.25", 3.25" deep x 8", all patented 5-8-17 and 5-27-19.

Back row: Fry Oven Glass, 9" x 13" oval baker with tab handles; *front row*: engraved Fry Oven Glass baker, 2.25" deep x 7" and an 8" trivet.

Six Fry Oven Glass custard cups, patented 5-8-17 and 5-27-19.

Three Fry Oven Glass pie/cake plates; *left to right:* 9.25", 6", 9", patented 5-8-17 and 5-27-19.

FLAMEWARE and Ovenware are featured in this 1937 advertisement.

An advertisement for PYREX® Ovenware, FLAMEWARE, and the very popular Colorware.

Fry's Heat Resisting Glass reamer with a 6.25" diameter.

CHAPTER ONE
PYREX® OVENWARE

Early efforts of the Corning scientists were commercial and scientific in nature. Items such as these insulators were produced.

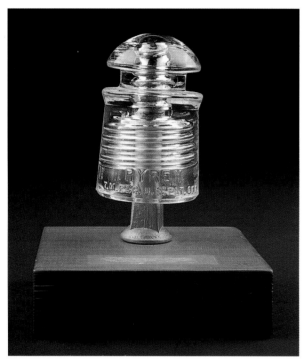

An insulator marked: "PYREX® T.M. REG. US. PAT. OFF. MADE IN U.S.A. PAT. APPD. FOR" and measuring 4".

An insulator marked: "PYREX® T.M. REG. U.S. PAT. OFF. MADE IN U.S.A.-453" and measuring 7.5".

Clear PYREX® Ovenware was introduced in 1915. According to Rogove and Steinhauer (*PYREX® By Corning: A Collector's Guide,* 1993), the identification numbers and original twelve items were as follows:

Number	Item
101	2 quart covered casserole
102	8.5" x 4.5" bread/loaf pan
103	1 quart covered casserole
104	1 pint covered casserole
201	8.5" pie plate
202	8" pie plate
301	7" shirred egg dish
302	5.5" shirred egg dish
322	6" x 8" oval au gratin dish
401	4" x 6" oval individual baker
402	3.5" custard cup
423	3" custard cup

Many of these items may still retain the original stamp, which looks like a backwards dollar signs above and below the word PYREX®.

This chapter presents clear PYREX® Ovenware, and several other transparent PYREX® items, in an alphabetical arrangement.

AU GRATIN DISHES

Au Gratin dishes are featured in both of these advertisements. Their appearance is a lot like a handled cake or pie plate. The handles, however, are molded with a slight elevation. By 1925, three sizes were available: No. 330, No. 331, and No. 332. Today they sell for $20-25 each.

An au gratin dish is featured in an advertisement from February 1925.

An au gratin dish serves breakfast in an advertisement from June 1925.

BASTERS

It is not difficult to locate good, virtually unused basters that have survived, with packaging, since their manufacture in the earlier part of the twentieth century. The ones presented here all have PYREX® glass tubes, but have been marketed by three different companies who added the rubber bulbs and packaging prior to marketing under their own names.

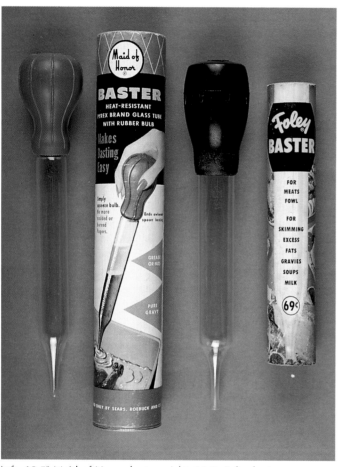

Left: 10.5" Maid of Honor baster; *right:* 10.5: Foley baster. $20-24 each.

Two Artbeck basters, both with 1946 copyrights. $20-24 each.

BOWLS

Round, clear mixing bowls were first produced in 1931, with the introduction of a 2 quart bowl. It was not until 1943 that nests of bowls were issued. The first clear sets had three bowls. Later, colored sets were introduced with four bowls each. Chapter Three presents an array of colorful PYREX® bowls.

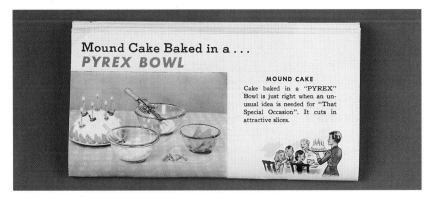

A catalogue from 1945 shows clear PYREX® mixing bowls.

Three bowls were only 95 cents.

Three round, clear mixing bowls. *Back:* 8.5" diameter, note the striped embellishments; *front left:* 5" diameter; *front right:* 6.75" diameter with 1 quart marking. $8-10 each.

Left: "Cinderella" handles for ease in holding and pouring. Bowls are 1.5 pints, 1.5 quarts and 3 quarts; *right:* bowls having measuring increments with a Swedish design in the following sizes level full: 1 cup, 3 cups, and 2 quarts. Each set of three $24-30.

Corning Glass Works advertised a "contemporary Swedish design with molded measures" in 1961. A set of three consisted of bowls with capacities of 1 cup, 1.5 pints, and 2 quarts.

Bowls with both handles having the same size were introduced in 1965. To augment sales, PYREX® bowls were also utilized in electric mixers manufactured by various contemporary companies.

Left: 1.5 quart bowl in a 3 quart bowl, $4-6 each; *right:* same 343 mold as the clear 1.5 quart bowl, $10-12.

Two bowls on left: both have a GE logo in the middle of the base, 9.25" diameter and 7.5" diameter; *right front:* 6.5" diameter marked: "PYREX® 25 MADE IN U.S.A. FOR WESTINGHOUSE;" *right back:* 8.75" diameter marked: "PYREX® MADE IN U.S.A. FOR KitchenAid". $8-10 each.

CAKE DISHES

The round cake dish was introduced in 1917. A square cake dish/utility pan followed and is featured in this chapter under "Utility Dishes." Note that there are two handles on the cake dishes pictured, while most pie plates have no handles.

A 1945 catalogue showing a PYREX® cake dish.

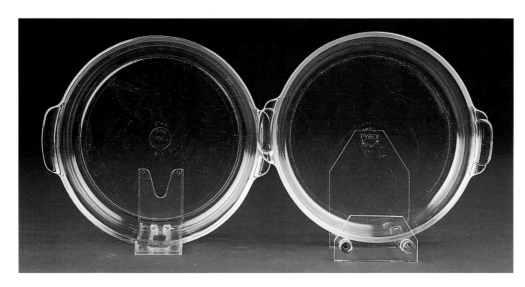

Two cake dishes.
$6-8 each.

Three cake dishes. $6-8 each.

Crisp brown undercrusts *just like the top*

A layer cake dish is shown in this June 1918 advertisement.

From freezing to boiling without breaking

A layer cake dish is shown in this May 1918 advertisement.

Featured in several PYREX® advertisements is a layer cake dish that has no handles. It was utilized as a cake stand in these advertisements, encouraging the homemaker to seek a variety of uses for her PYREX® items.

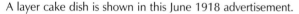

CASSEROLES

Three of the twelve original PYREX® Ovenware pieces were casseroles. Throughout Ovenware production, casseroles were manufactured either with lids having a center knob or flat lids (referred to as a "Utility Cover") having two handles that matched the handles of the base. Casseroles were also available without lids or handles and were called Pudding Dishes.

Casseroles with knob lids are almost endless. Their production originated in 1915 and continued over the years, with a variety of shape and size differentials. By 1922, 100 uniquely different transparent Ovenware items had been made. The first design had the lid rest just inside the rim of the base. Next came the "Victor" cover, which was a bit taller and rested on a rim molded onto the matching base. The creativity continued with further designs and modifications resulting in the utility cover in the 1930s.

Good Housekeeping Calls for PYREX

THIS is an era of PYREX. These wonderful baking and serving dishes are as necessary to the modern home as electric lights.

PYREX improves food — serves it more attractively and ends the drudgery of pot and pan scouring.

Every PYREX dish shows you the need for another, for *no home can have too much Pyrex.*

There are 100 styles and sizes of PYREX, from which to completely equip your home. Buy *your* Pyrex outfit from any dealer in housewares.

Pyrex Sales Division
CORNING GLASS WORKS
Corning, N.Y.
Originators and Patentees of Oven Glassware

No home can have too much *PYREX
Transparent Ovenware

In using advertisements see page 6 231

A round shallow baking dish or pudding dish is shown in the PYREX® advertisement.

How tempting food Looks in Pyrex

How much more satisfactory it is to serve food from a dainty dish like this than from the old-fashioned baking dishes. Every kind of food looks more appetizing in Pyrex.

And any food bakes better in Pyrex, too. Pyrex retains the heat and cooks the food more thoroughly and more quickly.

Pyrex is practical in every way. Every housewife appreciates how easy it is to keep Pyrex clean. It is guaranteed against oven breakage and will last indefinitely.

Try baking beans in Pyrex. You can watch them bake right through the dish. Practically everything you cook on top of the stove can be cooked better and more cheaply in the oven.

The largest manufacturers of technical glassware in the world perfected Pyrex after many years of experimenting. Ask any dealer or send for a booklet to the CORNING GLASS WORKS, *101 Tioga Ave., Corning, N.Y.*

PYREX

There is a Pyrex dish for every purpose—from 15c to $2.00

This October 1917 advertisement features a casserole and cover.

Four casseroles with lids. $15-18 each.

Original labels add $5 to the value of a covered casserole that would otherwise sell for $15-18 each.

Left: 2 quart covered casserole; *right:* 1 quart covered casserole. $15-18 each.

Two casseroles with utility lids. $15-18 each.

By 1936, PYREX® casseroles with utility covers were produced in 1 quart, 1.5 quart, 2 quart, and 3 quart sizes with prices ranging from $1.10-1.60. Such versatility had been previously unknown to American homemakers. The bases and lids could be used separately for baking, serving, or storing. Covers were also useful as tiles (trivets) or could be inverted and placed back on the base, thus creating a "Double Baker." The lids were often marked with mold numbers. Those shown are marked " 723 C."

This casserole has an 8.5" diameter. $15-18.

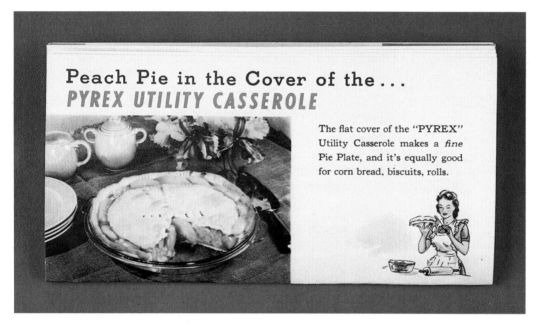

5 Layer Dinner • Baked and Served in the...
PYREX CASSEROLE

"PYREX" Casseroles come in one quart to three quart sizes—with flat or knobbed covers. And they stack well, too!

Use "PYREX" covered casseroles to carry hot or cold foods to picnics and church suppers.

All Photography by
Ayres A. Stevens - Corning Glass Works

A 1945 catalogue features the PYREX® casserole and two different lids.

Peach Pie in the Cover of the...
PYREX UTILITY CASSEROLE

The flat cover of the "PYREX" Utility Casserole makes a *fine* Pie Plate, and it's equally good for corn bread, biscuits, rolls.

The utility cover of a casserole is used as a pie plate.

Company Bread goes right to the table in its
PYREX BAKING DISH

This "Company Bread" is delicious as a breakfast sweet roll or as dessert at supper time. "PYREX" Ware keeps breads hot and tasty for second servings.

A PYREX® baking dish is used for serving, too. The PYREX® glass holds the heat keeping the food warm.

An advertisement from October 1927 includes a PYREX® casserole for $1.75.

There is other marking information worth noting. Ovenware items upon which the number begins with the digit 6 are items that originally sold as covered casseroles. Glassware with hyphenated digits, such as 026-686, were available with or without a lid.

Not pictured, but also made, were square casseroles like the No. 800 which came with a knob lid and the square pudding dish, No. 801.

CHILDREN'S OVENWARE

"The Pyrexette" was a miniature version of Mother's genuine PYREX® Ovenware. The six-piece set allowed the young lady of the house to practice the culinary arts alongside of her mother. This set, available from 1925-1929, included a casserole with a lid, bread pan, pudding or baking dish, pie plate, and two custard cups and retailed for $2.00.

The lid for a set of Pyrexette.

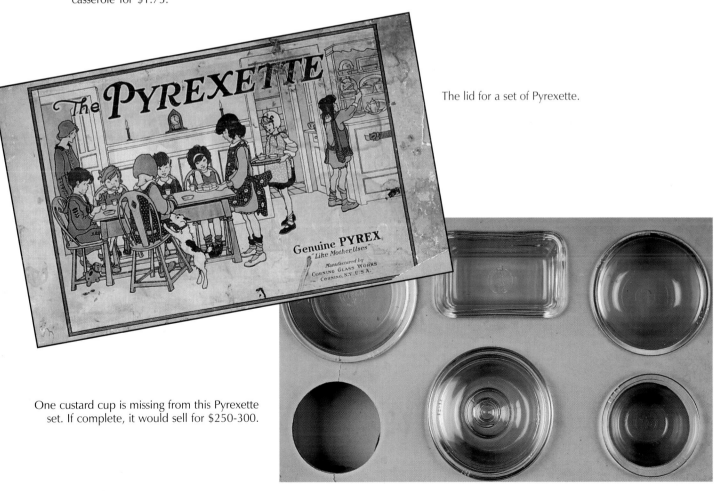

One custard cup is missing from this Pyrexette set. If complete, it would sell for $250-300.

CUSTARD CUPS

Since their introduction in 1915, PYREX® custard cups have continued to be easily recognizable items to most Americans. The sizes and styles have changed a bit, but their thoroughly useful design has not. Factor in their innate durability and the fact that most households bought sets rather than individual units, and these Ovenware pieces have stood and conquered the test of time.

In June 1928, a single custard cup sold for four cents. The introductory price of a three ounce custard cup in 1915 had been fifteen cents.

The Great Depression effected prices and PYREX® items cost less in the early 1930s than they did in the late 1920s. Note the rack for the custards shown in the top grouping. The rack alone is now worth $40-45.

More contemporary, but the custard cups are still a bargain. The scalloped edge on these custard cups was introduced in 1950. This set is now worth $20-25 as originally packaged.

Two sizes were originally produced in 1915 and by 1918 five varieties were available. Two more designs were added in 1921. As PYREX® Ovenware manufacturing continued, various sizes and styles were dropped, added, and occasionally reintroduced. The rimless design was begun in 1938 and the scalloped edge was introduced in 1950. Despite all of the design modifications, custard cups were usually marketed in sets of six.

A variety of custard cup styles and sizes. $3.50-5 each.

PYREX Custard Cup Set with 6 Custard Cups and a cooking rack. This design was advertised as "New style…lighter…daintier". Although the Custard Cups are easy to find the rack has become an elusive collectible. Original, unused sets are difficult to find. This one is pictured in the advertisement shown on page 29. As shown in box $75; the rack alone sells for $40-45. *Courtesy of Janice Johnston/Behind the Green Door*

A variety of custard cup styles and sizes. $3.50-5 each.

A variety of custard cup styles and sizes. $3.50-5 each.

A variety of custard cup styles and sizes. Note the engraved examples in the back row, having the French pattern. *Plain:* $3.50-5 each; *engraved:* $8-10 each.

Three custard cups in a rack with PYREX® in the center of the knobbed metal lids. This arrangement would allow use as a condiment server, egg poacher, or any suitable culinary task. $70-80.

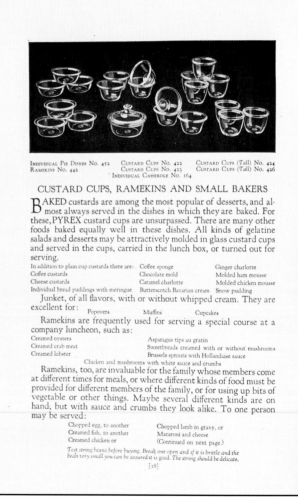

A 1925 listing of PYREX® custard cups, ramekins, and small bakers. "Ramekin" was used interchangeably with custard cup.

PYREX eight piece "Matched Set" featuring a casserole "Sweet and Low" and six custard cups "thin as table glass". This is set #145 which contains one, 1-1/2 qt. double duty casserole with a pie plate cover and six, 5 oz. custard cups. Original, unused sets are difficult to find. This one is pictured in the advertisement shown on page 29. Boxed as shown $85. *Courtesy of Janice Johnston/Behind the Green Door*

In 1942, three different custard cup arrangements were available, but all were offered in sets of six.

More glamorous uses of the custard cup, courtesy of Corning Glass Works in 1945.

The manufacturer publicized some uses for the large custard cups, also known as round utility dishes and small bakers in 1945.

DECORATED AND ENGRAVED OVENWARE

"Style RD" was Red Decorated glassware, produced in 1936 and 1937. The chemicals used to create this design were found to be poisonous and the line was discontinued. Today, these pieces are most prized among PYREX® collectors. They are even more popular than the lovely engraved pieces.

Engraved Ovenware was offered as early as 1918, with designs tending to be floral more frequently than geometric. Early catalogues mention the Fern, Spray, and Key designs, but presented here are other designs as well. The popularity of engraving peaked in the 1930s. By the 1940s, it was discontinued. As with other PYREX® items, engraved Ovenware was available in sets and individually. These highly decorative items, however, commanded higher prices. The Corning Glass Works publication *Getting the Most Out of Foods* stated, "Prices slightly higher than for corresponding plain units...fifty cents to seventy-five cents according to size of dish and amount of engraving."

Above: The 8.5" casserole in the back features Style RD and is valued at $100-120. The 7.5" and 8" casseroles in the front are worth $45-50 each.

Left: This grouping is engraved in the Spray design. Pie plate: $20-25; custard cups: $8-10 each; loaf pan: $20-25; squat teapot: $175-200; casserole: $45-50.

The covered baker on the right is engraved in the Fern design. $45-50 each.

These lids show the varieties of engravings one may find. When originally marketed, lids with engraving retailed for more than the same lid if plain. $20-25 each.

Engraved casseroles. $45-50 each.

Engraved casseroles. $45-50 each.

Engraved casserole without cradle. $45-50 each.

Engraved casseroles. $45-50 each.

Engraved casserole. $45-50.

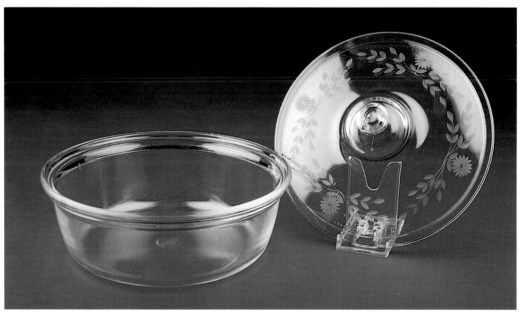

Engraved casserole without cradle, $25-30.

Engraved casserole. $25-30.

Engraved loaf pan. $25-30.

Engraved casserole, also known as a covered baker. $25-30.

Engraved pie plates. $20-25 each.

Engraved pie plate, $20-25; engraved ramekin, $8-10.

Engraved utility lids pictured with one base. Lids, $20-25 each; plain casserole base, $5.

Engraved utility lids pictured with one base. Lids, $20-25 each; plain casserole base, $5.

Engraved casserole on a difficult-to-find chrome base plate. $75-85.

Engraved well and tree meat platter with difficult-to-find chrome base plate. $50-60.

Matched grouping. Knob and utility lids, $20-25 each; plain casserole base, $5; teapot $175-200.

LOAF PANS

One of the twelve original Ovenware pieces from 1915, Item number 102, was an 8.5" x 4.5" loaf pan. A variety of sizes were developed, some having straight sides and some having sloping sides. Original loaf pans, also called bread pans and oblong open baking dishes, had no handles. Handles were later added.

Above: A September 1918 advertisement includes testimonies from delighted users of PYREX®.

Left: This advertisement from April 1918 explains the science responsible for the success of baking in a PYREX® loaf pan.

Four early loaf pans. Note the absence of any handles. $10-12 each.

Three loaf pans. Note the inclusion of handles. $8-10 each.

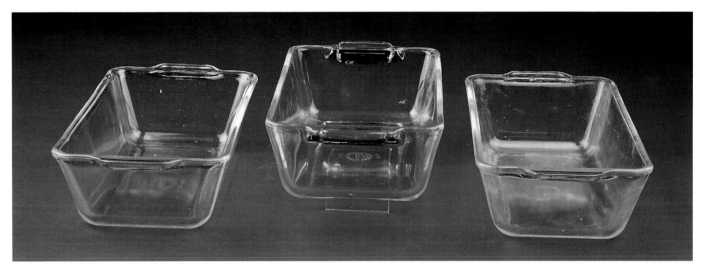

Three loaf pans. Note the inclusion of handles. $8-10 each.

A page from a 1945 PYREX® catalogue offers additional uses for the loaf pan.

MEASURING CUPS

Like the custard cup, the PYREX® measuring cup is probably a part of most American homes. And, like the custard cup, it is still manufactured today in nearly its original form. With the exception of the handle, few changes have been made to this measuring cup in the past fifty years. Measuring cups manufactured in the 1990s have a handle that is open at the bottom, but the earlier designs all had handles that curved back into and against the side of the cup.

The first PYREX® measuring cup was introduced in 1925 and featured dual spouts. The design of this fifty cent item was altered almost immediately and a single-spouted measuring cup was offered in 1926. Adjustments were made to the slope of the sides and the shape of the handle; but, by the early 1940s, these units evolved into forms most Americans readily recognize today.

During this period, two sizes dropped in price. In 1942, the one cup dry and one cup liquid measures both sold for fifteen cents apiece. The one pint liquid measure remained at fifty cents and the one quart measure had risen to seventy-five cents.

PYREX® measuring cups were durable and easy to read as the increments were printed in red. A variety of sizes were available: 8, 12, and 16 ounce liquid measures and 8 ounce dry measures.

This one quart measuring cup with the beater top is a highly desirable PYREX® collectible. The 5.25" measuring cup is marked: "FOR GENERAL HOUSEHOLD AND PHOTOGRAPHIC USE ONLY 532." The beater is marked, "FITS PYREX® NO. 532 ONE QUART MEASURE ANOTHER ANDROCK PRODUCT MADE IN UNITED STATES OF AMERICA PATENT NO. 2210810." $75-90.

One dry and four liquid measuring cups with the red markings introduced in 1941. Dry, $35-40; liquid, $20-25 each.

All five of these measuring cups were produced prior to 1941, when red markings began. $20-25 each.

A mold made in England measuring 5.25" across and 3" deep. $50-55.

MOLDS

There is only one example of a PYREX® mold that is presented in this book and it was made in England, not the United States. For American collectors it is an elusive piece of Ovenware that would surely enhance any collection.

Another view of the British-made PYREX® mold.

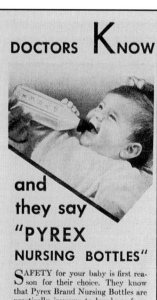

GONE—the old time worry of bottles that break in heating

In the 2 shapes doctors approve—the narrow neck and the wide open top

Plunge a cold bottle into boiling water or cool a hot bottle in icy water without fear of breaking!

HERE are bottles you can heat or cool as rapidly as you like without their breaking!

For PYREX nursing bottles are made especially to resist all extreme or sudden temperature shocks.

These heat-proof nursing bottles are six-sided so they will not roll or slip from your grasp; angles are broadly rounded off—smooth inside for easy cleaning; graduations are plainly marked.

PYREX nursing bottles come in the two shapes that doctors approve—*narrow neck and wide open top*—in 8-oz. size.

Order enough from your druggist for a full day's feeding and banish forever the worry of bottles that break in heating! Made by the makers of PYREX ovenware. Corning Glass Works, Corning, N. Y.

PYREX
T M REG US PAT OFF
NURSING BOTTLES

DOCTORS Know
and they say "PYREX NURSING BOTTLES"

SAFETY for your baby is first reason for their choice. They know that Pyrex Brand Nursing Bottles are practically immune to breakage from heat or cold. They protect your baby against the dangers of bottles cracked or broken in heating or in sterilizing.

And you'll enjoy using "Pyrex" Nursing Bottles because they're comfortable to hold, easy to clean, and plainly marked for quick, accurate measuring.

Two sizes . . . 8-oz. with narrow neck or wide mouth, 25¢; and new 4-oz., narrow neck, 15¢.

"Pyrex" is the registered trade-mark of Corning Glass Works Corning, N. Y., and indicates their brand of resistant glass. These prices for the U. S. only.

NURSING BOTTLES

Nursing bottles are cross-collectibles also sought by those collecting baby and children's items. The competition for, and interest in, nursing bottles is greater than for some of the cook ware.

Eight ounce nursing bottles were first available in a narrow neck and wide mouth design and sold for twenty-five cents apiece. The four ounce narrow neck was later added and finally the four ounce wide neck. The last design change was the threaded top for screwing on and unscrewing the nipple ring. The "evenflo" sleeves shown in the pictures are dated 1950.

An advertisement, when only the eight ounce nursing bottle was available.

An advertisement, now including the new four ounce nursing bottle.

A variety of nursing bottles. Narrow neck, 8 oz., $20-25; screw tops, $10-12 each. Add $10 for original packaging.

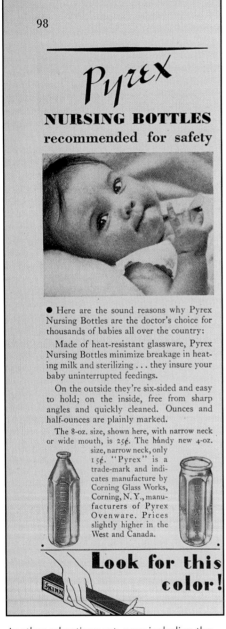
Another advertisement, now including the new four ounce nursing bottle

A page from "Getting the Most Out of Food" touting the virtues of the PYREX® nursing bottle.

A variety of nursing bottles. Narrow neck, 4 oz., $20-25; screw tops, $10-12 each; wide mouths, $25-30 each. Add $10 for original packaging.

Pie birds, $50-60 each.

PIE BIRDS

Both of the pie birds pictured are from Australia, not the United States. The small, 2" pie bird is unmarked. The 2.5" pie bird reads: "PYREX® BRAND."

Pie birds are inserted through the top crust of a pie prior to baking. The pie bird acts as a vent allowing steam to escape during the baking process and eliminating the mess from a leaking pie.

PIE PLATES

An eight inch and eight and a half inch pie plate were each among the original twelve PYREX® ovenware items offered. These were so well received that variations flourished. By 1920 there were wide rim pie plates in every inch increment from five inches through eleven inches. Certain sizes were also offered with narrow rims. From 1917-1938, there were even hexagonal pie plates.

8.5" pie plate marked 208 1-1/2 inch L-19. Found in Canada it is an advertising piece marked Compliments of Traquair Hardware, Exeter. $30.

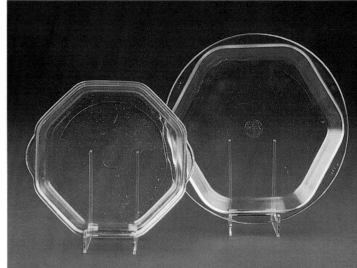

7.5" and 10" hexagonal pie plates. The speckled appearance is due to imperfections in the glass. $18-20 each.

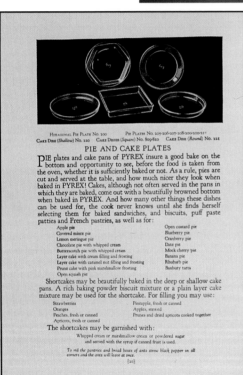

A 1925 publication shows a variety of PYREX® pie plates.

Three pie plates with wide rims. $8-10 each.

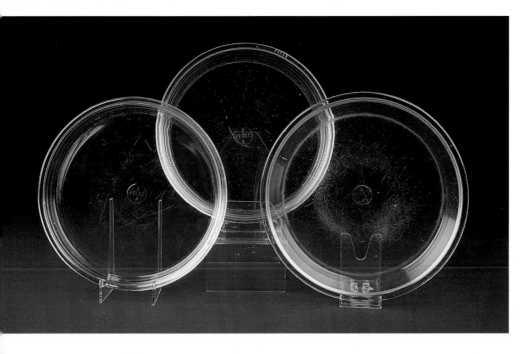

Three pie plates with wide rims.
$8-10 each.

Four pie plates with wide rims.
$8-10 each.

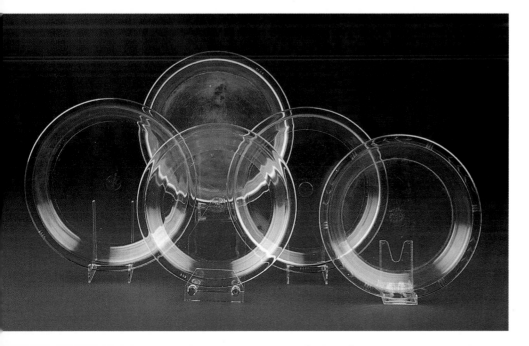

Five pie plates with wide rims.
$8-10 each, except engraved
pie plate on right, $20-25.

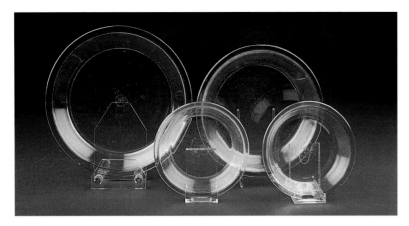

Four pie plates with wide rims. $8-10 each.

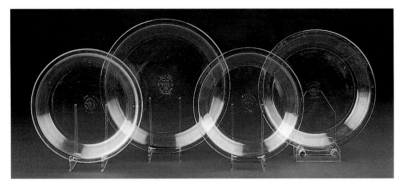

Four pie plates with wide rims. $8-10 each.

Ever conscious of the need to create new merchandise, the ten-inch "Flavor-Saver Pie Plate" was introduced by the Corning Glass Works in 1943. The fluted-edged design was advertised to "keep *all* the juice and flavor in your pies." Like many previous Ovenware items, this was so popular that other sizes were produced. By 1945 the "Flavor-Saver" was also available in eight and nine inch diameters.

PYREX "Blue Diamond" Gift Set. Packaged to be a wedding, Christmas, Valentine's Day, or Anniversary present. This No. 295 set comes complete with: 1-No. 516 Measuring Cup-16 oz.; 1-No. 683 Casserole with Utility Cover-52 oz.; 1-No. 228 Flavor Saver Pie Plate-9 in.; 1-No. 232 Utility Disk-12-1/2"x8"x2"; 6-No. 462 Custard Cups-5 oz.; 1-Wire Custard Cup Rack. $75-100. *Courtesy of Janice Johnston/Behind the Green Door*

An advertisement for the "Flavor Saver" pie plate.

This advertisement introduced the "Flavor Saver" pie plate to the American homemaker.

This page from a 1945 catalogue lists the "Flavor Saver's" three sizes.

Also from a 1945 catalogue, the price of only the ten inch pie plate is shown, listed at forty-five cents.

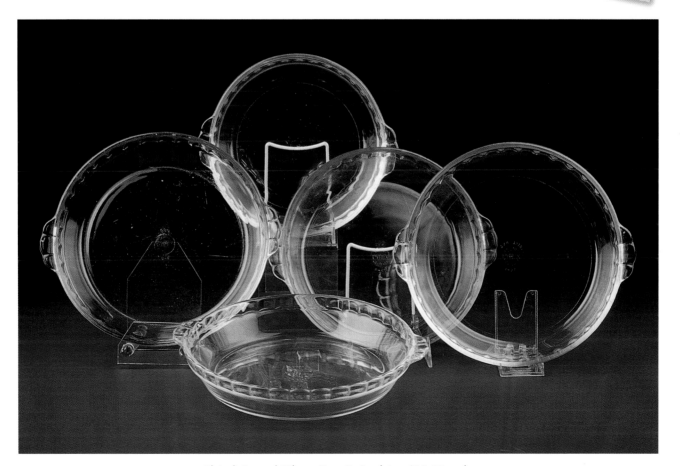

Fluted-rimmed "Flavor Saver" pie plates. $10-15 each.

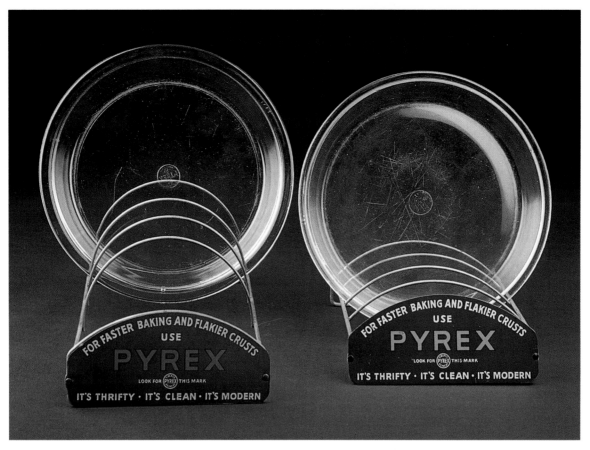

Two store racks to display and sell PYREX® pie plates. (Rack on left courtesy of L.E. Fawber and Thomas Dibeler.) $125-150 each.

PYREX® pie plates were so durable that many still exist today. Scratches effect the value, therefore the prices quoted are for examples in excellent condition. Some of the pie plates shown do have scratching and would be worth less than the prices presented in the captions. Published in 1953, the cookbook *PYREX® Prize Recipes* provides exacting directions and ingredients for crust fitting the following PYREX® pie plates: 5.5", 7.5", 8.5", 9.5", and 10.5", plus the "Flavor-Saver Pie Plate."

PLATTERS

The first oval platters were introduced in 1921. Platters No. 313 and 315 were available by 1925 and the original two were discontinued in 1926. These handy, oversized dishes in two different sizes (about 12" long and about 15" long) were designed not only to serve but to bake and also retain the heat of cooked food. The smaller platter sold for $1.15 and the larger one for $2.00.

The successful acceptance of these platters by the American housewife led to other platters. Well and tree platters were designed to drain juices away from prepared items and were available until 1950, with an initial selling price of $2.25. Like many Ovenware items, the price dropped and the platter sold for $1.85 in 1936. Platters were produced with engraved embellishments and with chrome under plates. They were also marketed as chafing dishes with candles as the heat source.

The nature of their use made platters susceptible to knife scratching. The prices presented are for items in excellent condition.

PLATTER No. 313   PLATTER No. 315   TILE No. 706   TRAY No. 710

PLATTERS AND TRAYS

IF you have ever tried to lift a large baked fish from pan to serving dish without breaking the fish, you will, without hesitation, welcome the platter which makes the transfer unnecessary. Besides the PYREX platter keeps the fish hot for a long time.

Not only for fish, but for cooking and serving steaks, chops and other meats, PYREX not only bakes them more thoroughly and tenderly, but keeps them hot during the entire meal. The fastidious hostess can well appreciate this advantage.

Every home needs a PYREX Platter.

PYREX platters may be used instead of planks with a potato border and a garnish of vegetables around the meat or fish. This is especially practical in the small family.

There are two sizes, to meet the needs of large and small families.

The trays are attractive both as serving trays and as cooky sheets.

Suggestions for using PYREX platters.

Baked Stuffed Haddock	Halibut with peppers
Baked Mackerel with milk or cream	Lemon Sole
Baked Finnan haddie	Codfish Puff
Baked fish with oyster stuffing	Baked salt mackerel
Shad roe with brown sauce	Spinach with fillets of sole
Codfish soufflé	Pompano with Paprika Sauce
Whitefish with shrimps	Finnan haddie baked with white sauce and small
Fish baked with tiny tomatoes	potatoes

The PYREX Trays Make Admirable Cooky Sheets for

Molasses cookies	Dropped cookies	Turnovers
Sugar cookies	Chocolate cookies	Macaroons
	Ginger cookies	

The PYREX trays are well adapted to use as sandwich trays, also for tea service and used under a casserole or pudding dish.

When boiled ham is taken from the hot water, dip it immediately in cold water for a moment to make the fat firm and white.

[24]

This page from a 1925 publication shows two PYREX® platters.

Note the decorative handles on the platter at right. *Left*: $10-15; *right*: $18-20.

A well and tree platter fits into a metal frame to create a chafing dish.
In 1945, the platter without the frame sold for $1.50. $25-30.

A well and tree planter was advertised at $1.85.

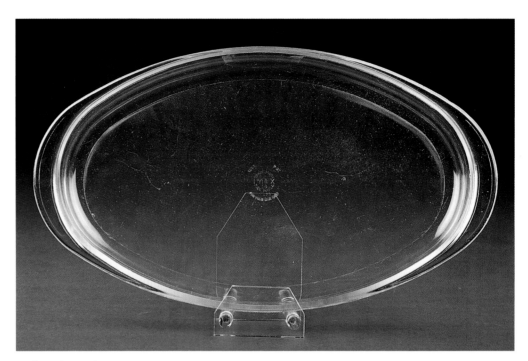

A plain platter. $10-15.

The same platter with embellishments. As this style is not in favor with today's collectors, the value is not enhanced by the extra details.

REAMERS

There is only one example of a PYREX® reamer in this book. These two-part juicers are difficult to find.

A PYREX® reamer. $75-85.

REFRIGERATOR DISHES

This section is devoted to clear Ovenware refrigerator dishes. Colorful PYREX® refrigerator dishes are presented in Chapter Three.

The first refrigerator sets were marketed in 1925 and continued in one form or another until the popular colored sets completely overtook the originals in 1952. The first set is shown in a 1925 catalogue page. The cleverly thought-out design enabled homemakers to efficiently utilize ice box space. They were stackable and had square corners to tightly fit the limited interior space of an ice box. One of the best features was the simple fact that this was PYREX® Ovenware. Therefore the contents could be stored, baked, reheated, and served in these same convenient containers.

As with other successful lines, the refrigerator dish evolved. Different lids, sizes, and shapes were developed. By 1930, there were five sizes: 5" x 9" x 2", 5" x 9" x 3", 6" x 6" x 2", 6" x 6" x 3", and the newest: 5 5/8" x 10 5/8" x 3 3/8". Prices ran from $.95 to $2.50 for the latest model. Round dishes, which came later, were less popular and their manufacture was terminated in 1939 while the rectangular, flat-lidded refrigerator dish remained.

A page from a 1925 catalogue.

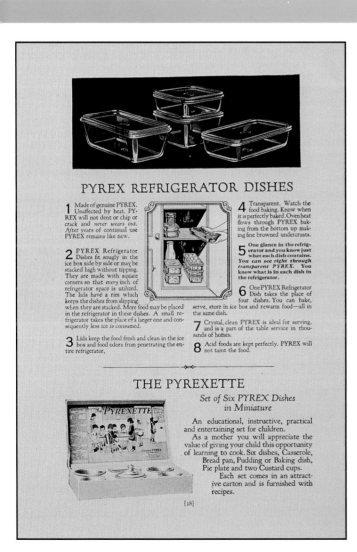

51

The refrigerator dishes on the left and in the center are the earliest. The example on the right shows a newer cover design. $8-15 each.

The use of round refrigerator dishes was short lived. Today's collectors of clear PYREX® prefer this style to the clear rectangular refrigerator dishes. $8-15 each

ROASTERS

The first roasters sold by Corning Glass Works had aluminum bases manufactured by other companies and PYREX® Ovenware lids. These $5.00 ($5.50 in the western states) items appeared in the marketplace in the mid-1920s and were advertised as PYREX® roasters. It was recommended to the consumer that the durable PYREX® cover could also be used as a serving platter.

All-glass roasters were created in the early 1950s, having two identical pieces resting together. Advertising suggested that either part could be used individually or the unit could be kept together. Anchor Hocking had already created an all-glass roaster by this time, so it was inevitable that a PYREX® roaster would follow. PYREX® roasters were made round, oval, and eventually open (having no lids). This line was discontinued in the mid-1960s.

Note that both halves of this three quart roaster are identical. Overall dimensions are 15.5" x 5.5". $40-50.

Here is a good comparison: the rounded lid on the unit on the left reveals that this is a roaster. The items on the right are casseroles with utility lids. Roaster: $40-50; casseroles with utility lids: $15-20 each.

Both of these PYREX® roasters are from England. The roaster on the left is 11" x 10" x 8" and has handles that line up in an exact configuration. The roaster on the right is 11" x 10.25" x 6". $40-50 each.

ROLLING PINS

Collectors of kitchenware know how elusive PYREX® rolling pins are, and both of the examples presented here are from England. By having removable end pieces, these rolling pins were designed to act as reservoirs for cold water or ice. This technique for working dough was popular among bakers and homemakers.

Two English rolling pins. $60-75 each.

SHIRRED EGG DISHES

Among the original Ovenware items were 5.5" and 7" shirred egg dishes. These oval servers had decorative tab handles on two sides. Very little documentation exists on these elusive serving platters. One can deduce that they were not popular and were discontinued.

The 1952 model of the 7" skillet was also designed to be a shirred egg dish. There are no shirred egg dishes photographed in this reference.

SPECIAL DISHES

PYREX® Ovenware had an assortment of specialty items which Corning Glass Works referred to as "Special Dishes" in a 1925 publication. The first of these is the Mushroom Dish which is shown in the reprint of this catalogue page. The intended use of this 2-part item was for baking mushrooms; however, it was certainly not limited to this use.

Special Dishes are shown in a Corning Glass Works publication from 1925.

One of the challenges of cooking and baking in the early part of the twentieth century was having all of the items for a meal ready to serve at the same time. PYREX® Ovenware was designed to help homemakers overcome this difficulty. The Double Compartment Baking Dish, which debuted in 1922, made it possible for two items to go into, and thus be removed from, the oven simultaneously. Also pictured are 3-part Grill plates. Advertisements reminded homemakers that leftover meats and vegetables could be reheated in a $1.25 sectional plate, so residential use followed to a lesser extent. Today's collectors give this divided plate mixed reviews.

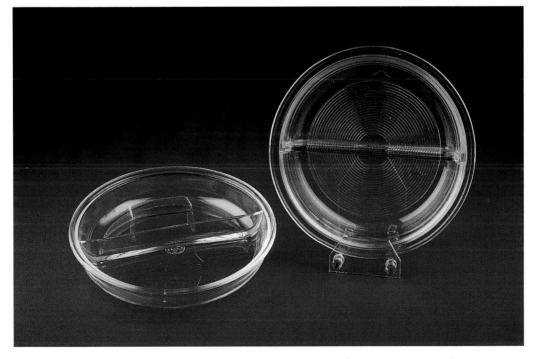

Double Compartment Baking Dishes, both having 10" diameters. $15-18 each.

Double Compartment Baking Dish in a copper liner. $35-45.

Prior to PYREX® Ovenware Bean Pots, beans were baked in earthenware containers. PYREX® Bean Pots, first offered in 1917, were touted as being much more attractive, as well as being usable for many other side dishes. By 1921 they were available in 1 pint, 1 quart, and 2 quart sizes, but were eventually discontinued in the late 1930s.

Bean pot, 6" x 6". $40-50.

10.5" and 8.25" Sectional Plates. Smaller plate is marked: "PYREX® BRAND GLASSWARE MADE IN U.S.A. FOR MEALPACK." $15-18 each.

TEAPOTS

Unlike FLAMEWARE teapots (see Chapter Two), Ovenware teapots would not tolerate direct heat from a stove top. However, as Americans had come to expect from PYREX® glassware, these teapots were capable of handling extreme temperatures and hot water could be poured into the teapot.

The earliest models, begun in 1922, were completely glass. Three distinct designs were offered as: round shape, squat shape, and tall shape (and shared the same sizes and prices). Three-cup teapots sold for $2.50, four-cup teapots were $3.00, and six-cup teapots cost $3.50.

The advantages of using one of these PYREX® teapots were clearly delineated in *Expert's Book on Better Cooking* in 1925: "It is always possible to see how strong the tea is. It is easy to see how much tea there is and if someone may have a second or third cup. The tea pot can be easily and thoroughly cleaned. The spouts pour freely. The handles remain cold while the body of the pot stays hot. The double rim on the lids prevents their falling off when the tea is poured. There can be no harmful action of the tannin in the tea upon the inside of the tea pot. Boiling water will not crack them."

Changes began to occur in the mid-1920s. The tall teapot was eliminated. Single cup units were made in the round design and sold for $2.25, and engraving was now available on the squat teapot. Other manufacturers began to purchase PYREX® teapots, adding their own touches to the design, including features such as metal lids. (This was a common practice of this era. Companies also purchased items from other glass companies, such as sugar bowls and cereal bowls, and manufactured metal covers for these as well.)

In the mid-1930s, teapots—sold also as beverage servers for a greater mass appeal—were offered in one-cup and four-cup sizes. Plastic and chrome plated handles were used, and embellishments to the glass were added.

As the popularity of FLAMEWARE increased, consumer demand for these teapots waned. By the 1940s, PYREX® Ovenware teapots were no longer being produced, except for a brief resurrection in the 1960s.

Three round teapots, $125-150 each and one squat teapot, $175-200.

Three teapots or beverage servers. Note: the two on the sides are identical except for the engraving; center one has glass lid. *Left to right:* $30-40, $50-60, $60-70.

Left to right: Squat teapot with engraving and metal additions, $175-200; round teapot with engraving and metal additions, $175-200; squat teapot with 1960s handle, $60-75; teapot or beverage server from the 1930s, note the glass cover and ebony black handle, $50-65.

Three teapots. *Left and middle:* "PYREX® Brand for teamakers, inc.," $30-40; *right:* stainless steel with PYREX® glass interior marked "teamakers, inc. Model 6600," $50-60.

One cup teapot or beverage servers. $25-35 each.

One cup teapot or beverage server as originally packaged. $35-45.

Four one cup teapots. *Back left*: 5.75" tall with snowflake embellishments marked: "PYREX® MADE IN U.S.A."; *front left*: 4" tall with same mark as unit in back left; *back right*: 4" tall marked: "PYREX® 802 CORNING NY, USA USE WITH WIRE GRID ON ELECTRIC RANGE"; *front right*: 3.5" tall with a lid designed to hold a tea bag and marked: "PYREX®WARE FOR teamakers ANOTHER EKCO PRODUCT 66102 2 CUP." $25-35 each.

TRAYS OR TILES

Round 10" trays with handles were available as early as 1917 and were intended for serving. Within three years, trays were offered in two sizes, with a third option available by 1922. At this point they were listed in catalogues as "Trays or Tiles" and sold for fifty cents, seventy-five cents, or a dollar, depending on size. By 1925, "tiles" referred specifically to the smaller trays, such as the one pictured, and the "trays" label was reserved exclusively for larger items.

To mark the twenty-fifth anniversary of PYREX® Ovenware in 1940, a monogrammed "table saver" was available for thirty-five cents and a label from a PYREX® dish. Suggested uses for this item included: hot dish holder, coaster, ashtray (turn it upside down), and server (again use it upside down).

Two tiles. *Left*: 6" diameter with small tab handles; *right*: 6.25" and marked PYREX® on bottom edge. $25-30 each.

UTILITY DISHES

This category encompasses what Corning Glass Works described in a 1925 publication to be "bread, biscuit, and utility pans." These rectangular and square Ovenware items were offered at various sizes, shapes, and prices, although Corning Glass Works later narrowed this listing to have only two pieces.

Advertising campaigns reminded homemakers of the vast array of uses they had from entrees to desserts and by 1925 the 10-1/2" x 6- 1/2" x 2" sold for $1.15 and the 12-5/8" x 8-1/8" x 2" sold for $2.00. However, PYREX® prices dropped; by 1928 the smaller of these was available for one dollar, by 1932 only seventy-five cents, and by 1942 it was a bargain at fifty cents. In 1945 this category was reduced to a one quart and a two quart dish.

Only one and two quart utility dishes are mentioned in this 1945 catalogue.

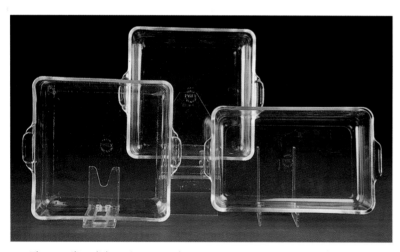

Three utility dishes. $8-12 each.

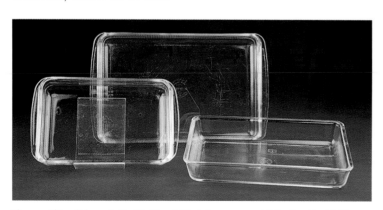

Three utility dishes. *Left:* 11.5" x 6.5", 1.5 quarts; *middle (back):* 15.5" x 9", marked "FOR BAKING ONLY"; *right:* 12.5" x 8". $8-12 each.

The advertised PYREX® would cost fifty cents.

The "BUFFET-MASTER" warmer/server has an aluminum exterior.
The 6" x 4" glass receptacles are PYREX®. $125-150.

WARMING DISHES

These buffet servers have PYREX® ovenware receptacles. Although they will help to keep cold foods cool, they were particularly useful for maintaining the temperatures of warm dishes. Each unit has three containers in which to hold prepared items. Complete, usable sets as pictured are not easy to find. As with any older kitchen collectible, it is easy for parts to get misplaced.

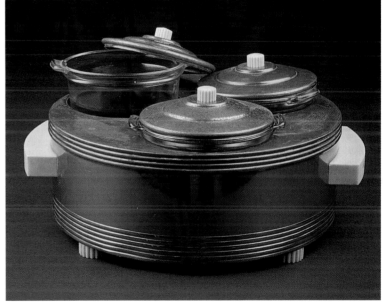

This buffet server has a copper exterior with PYREX® receptacles that are 5.25" x 4.5". $125-150.

Tags for the "BUFFET-MASTER."

A FINAL LOOK AT PYREX® OVENWARE

Prior to the creation of PYREX® Ovenware, homemakers utilized earthenware and metals for cooking, serving, and storing foods. This new invention allowed women to cook a complete meal at one time, serve with a new level of creativity, and store in an efficient manner, using dishes that allowed one to see what was being saved.

As PYREX® became enthusiastically accepted, the developers of Ovenware continued to meet the needs of American women by offering even more options at even lower prices. One Ovenware line that was particularly lovely was the "tulip" design that was added to some Ovenware, probably in the mid-1930s. Available in red and yellow, few of the tulip designs were made and even fewer survived the passing of use and time. The prices shown are for glassware that has maintained the original brightness.

Covered casserole: $75-80; round cake dish: $50-60; custard cups: $25-30 each; bowls: $50-60 each; loaf pan: $50-60.

CHAPTER TWO

PYREX® FLAMEWARE

Scientists at Corning Glass Works were continually striving to create newer and better products. From this research came FLAMEWARE, a wonderfully durable line of glassware designed to be used directly on the stove. Introduced in 1936, the first base pieces were manufactured with a bluish cast and were covered with clear lids. This distinctive coloration gives Flameware its own specific characteristic, distinguishing it from PYREX® Ovenware. Within ten years of its introduction, however, all FLAMEWARE pieces were manufactured in clear, uncolored glass. FLAMEWARE was produced until 1979.

During the first decade of production, the manufacturer's mark—one of five logos having flames and the word PYREX®—was stamped in green ink rather than molded into the glass. Many of the marks have been worn away with the passing of time and years of use.

Compared to PYREX® Ovenware, there are not many categories of PYREX® FLAMEWARE. However, as one explores this area, one finds that the ability to serve a perfect cup of coffee motivated the designers to create a huge number of FLAMEWARE items. American consumers are revisiting the pleasures of a delicious cup of coffee, and FLAMEWARE coffee makers have become highly collectible.

It is important to consider American culture and womens' reality at this point in time. Most American women were homemakers. Their daily routine was expected to be largely centered in the kitchen and around pleasing a working husband. Advertisements specifically targeted the joys and pleasures one would experience giving, getting, and using PYREX® products that would enhance a woman's culinary abilities. How best for a loving wife to say, "I love you?" But of course, with a perfectly prepared and presented meal and a satisfyingly delicious cup of coffee. This chapter presents PYREX® FLAMEWARE, and a few other treasures, in an alphabetical arrangement.

An advertisement from the 1940s.

An advertisement from the 1940s.

COFFEE MAKERS - INTRODUCTION

As the twentieth century continued, the options for brewing the ultimate cup of coffee broadened and narrowed. First they broadened as the equipment became more complicated and more ornate, with more pieces. Then life (and coffee making) simplified. American women became an integral part of the work force and domestic chores simply had to take less time and energy. As a reflection of changing society, at-home coffee production also changed and streamlined into one of the easiest procedures of all: instant coffee. Ever on the cutting edge of consumer needs, PYREX® glassware was a part of this evolution.

The front of a PYREX® brochure illustrated coffee making options.

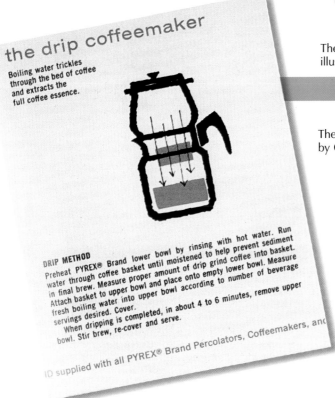

The drip coffee maker explained by Corning Glass Works.

COFFEE MAKERS -
THE DRIP COFFEE MAKER

The PYREX® brochure explains this process clearly and succinctly: "Boiling water trickles through the bed of coffee and extracts the full coffee essence." The brewing liquid permeates the central filtration and grounds to fill the bottom pot. The bottom unit separates and becomes the serving piece, using the lid from the upper section.

A six cup drip coffee maker, about 11" tall. $60-75.

COFFEE MAKERS - INSTANT COFFEE

The very nature of PYREX® glassware made their products absolutely perfect for instant coffee. The glass was able to tolerate the extreme temperature of the boiling water needed for a pot of instant coffee. Carafes and carafe-like containers resulted. One could place the carafe directly on the stove—although sometimes the manufacturer recommended placing a grid in between the stove top and the glassware—to heat the water. Alternatively, boiling water could be placed in the carafe and the coffee then added. There are other carafes in Chapter Three, as these were later offerings. The same glassware that successfully served steaming hot liquids also provided a lovely way to serve juices and other chilled beverages.

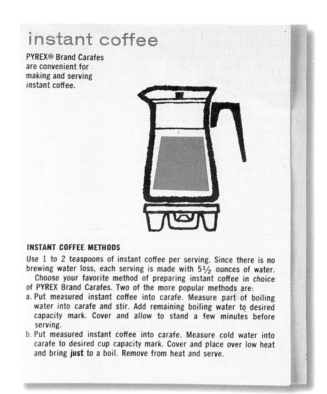

instant coffee

PYREX® Brand Carafes are convenient for making and serving instant coffee.

INSTANT COFFEE METHODS

Use 1 to 2 teaspoons of instant coffee per serving. Since there is no brewing water loss, each serving is made with 5½ ounces of water.
  Choose your favorite method of preparing instant coffee in choice of PYREX Brand Carafes. Two of the more popular methods are:
a. Put measured instant coffee into carafe. Measure part of boiling water into carafe and stir. Add remaining boiling water to desired capacity mark. Cover and allow to stand a few minutes before serving.
b. Put measured instant coffee into carafe. Measure cold water into carafe to desired cup capacity mark. Cover and place over low heat and bring **just** to a boil. Remove from heat and serve.

Instant coffee making explained by Corning Glass Works.

A ten ounce purchase of Instant Maxwell House Coffee provided the consumer with a free 8.5" PYREX® carafe in the mid-to-late 1960s. $20-25 as shown with labels.

A decorative instant coffee carafe.
$15-20.

Two early percolators with smaller flanges (knobs). $60-75 each.

COFFEE MAKERS - THE PERCOLATOR

This section is divided into two parts. The first illustrates true FLAMEWARE coffee percolators and their "descendants." The second section shows interesting coffee percolators with genuine PYREX® parts.

A coffee percolator may be one of the most recognizable coffee makers of all. The aroma of perking coffee is one many adults find extremely pleasurable and memorable. The directions provided by Corning Glass Works indicate that one pot of perked coffee would take about 6-8 minutes. During that time, the wonderful, anticipatory scent of coffee fills a kitchen.

FLAMEWARE six- and nine-cup percolators followed the introduction of saucepans and double boilers by several years. Just as a piece of PYREX® Ovenware was often capable of being utilized for a variety of tasks, so it is true with FLAMEWARE percolators. Once the tube (pump) and basket are removed, one has a saucepan! Percolator development was just a natural step in the process of providing options to the consumer.

During the thirtysome years FLAMEWARE percolators were manufactured, many subtle changes took place. Percolator lids were not the same as saucepan lids. These had smaller knobs (flanges) that eventually got larger. Handle styles and handle materials also varied. An elusive wooden-handled percolator was made during World War II.

the percolator

Hot water bubbles up through a tube, spraying gently over the ground coffee. As it seeps through the coffee, the flavor is extracted.

PERCOLATOR METHOD
The PYREX® Brand Percolator has beverage cup markings for easy measuring. Measure water into percolator according to number of servings of coffee desired. (Water level should not touch the bottom of the coffee basket.)
To help prevent sediment in brew, run water through the percolator basket before adding coffee. Measure proper amount of percolator or regular grind of coffee into the basket.
Insert basket assembly into percolator. Cover. Place over direct heat. When perking begins, use only enough heat to perk gently for 6 to 8 minutes. Coffee flavor is best if not allowed to boil. Coffee may be served more easily if basket assembly is removed before pouring.
Your PYREX Brand Percolator has a no-drip pouring lip for easy serving.

ALWAYS use the HEAT SPREADER GR

Corning Glass Works explains the percolator.

Three percolators with larger flanges. $60-75 each.

Two decorative percolators in two different sizes. $60-75 each.

A case of PYREX® parts. $100-125.

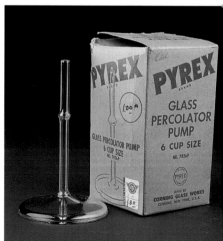

An unused pump. $20-25.

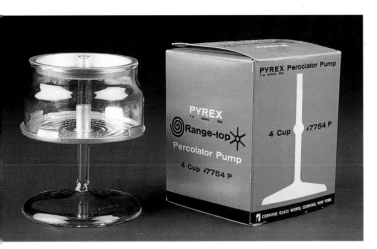

A newer, unused pump. The "Range-top" line is from the 1960s. $18-20.

A late 1940s advertisement.

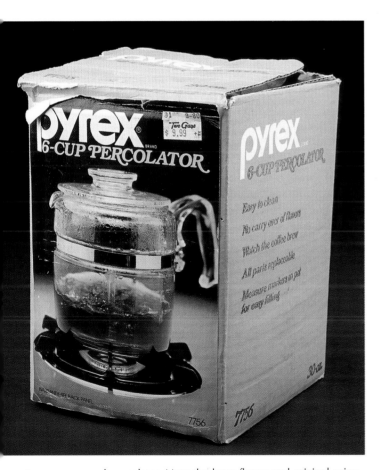

A newer, unused percolator. Note the large flange and original price of $9.99. $30-35.

Range Top Ware

Available in: 1 Qt., 1½ Qt. and 2 Qt. Covered Saucepans,
1½ Qt. Double Boiler, 6 Cup Teapot, 4 Cup, 6 Cup and
9 Cup Percolators.

A page from a PYREX® brochure discusses
Range Top Ware percolators.

Coffee perked in **PYREX** WARE ® tastes *better!*

Be a better cook

A late 1940s advertisement.

Christmas shopping? Look at these!

See these wonderful gifts—and dozens more—at your nearest Pyrex Ware counter! Pyrex Ware is an all-year joy for everyone who cooks!

Just out! New PYREX Hostess Set!

PYREX FLAMEWARE for top-of-stove cooking

PYREX OVENWARE for baking and roasting

PYREX WARE
A Product of
CORNING GLASS WORKS

An early 1950s advertisement indicating sizes and prices of percolators.

You taste the coffee... not the coffeepot... when you brew it in glass

PYREX® WARE
A PRODUCT OF CORNING

An early 1960s advertisement.

Above left: PYREX Flameware insert for double boiler. The insert indicates double boilers are "fine for preparing cereals, baby foods, etc., bottom is a handy sauce pan". Right: Range-tech insert for double boiler. Note the handle design is similar to that found on some PYREX cookware. As a collectible, the value lies in the fact that the original paperwork has survived. As shown in unused condition, $25-30. *Courtesy of Janice Johnston/Behind the Green Door*

PYREX® glassware was so durable and dependable, other companies used this glassware in their own products. An assortment of percolators is presented here.

Two British aluminum percolators with PYREX® 955 percolator tops. Both are marked the same: "J210 MADE BY N.C.J. LTD. AT REGD SONA CHROME THE ALUMINUM WORKS STRATFORD-ON-AVON ENGLAND." $100-125 each.

A 13" electric percolator with a Bakelite handle marked: "FOREMAN BROS. INC. BROOKLYN, NY" having a PYREX® percolator top. $100-125.

A "4 MAN COFFEE MAID" set having a PYREX® lining in the percolator. This Foreman 4 Family Inc. product from the 1930s is pictured with a 17.5" x 11" chrome tray and matching accessories. Missing is a 3-slice toast rack which would also be chrome. The handles and feet are black Bakelite. If complete, $300-350.

COFFEE MAKERS –
THE VACUUM COFFEE MAKER

The name of this type of coffee maker was derived from the vacuum that is formed during the brewing process. The procedure is explained by Corning Glass Works as: "Steam from boiling water creates pressure which forces water into the PYREX® brand bowl, where it gently bubbles through the ground coffee. When the lower bowl cools, a vacuum is created and pulls the brew through a filter into the lower bowl."

The first groupings of vacuum coffee makers are PYREX®. As with other PYREX® glasswares, these evolved and changed. Handle and lid styles were subtly altered and their materials changed. Decorative embellishments were also added to the glass, later to be removed.

the vacuum coffeemaker

Steam from boiling water creates pressure which forces water into the PYREX® Brand top bowl, where it gently bubbles through the ground coffee. When the lower bowl cools, a vacuum is created and pulls the brew through a filter into the lower bowl.

VACUUM METHOD

Measure water into lower bowl according to number of beverage servings desired. Place filter in upper bowl. Measure proper amount of fine grind coffee into the upper bowl. Insert upper bowl into lower bowl using a slight twist to insure a seal. Place over direct heat. When nearly all water rises into upper bowl, remove from heat, stir brew well. Brew should return to lower bowl in about 3 minutes.

When brew returns to lower bowl, remove upper bowl. Serve.

Carafes when using on electric ranges.

An explanation of the vacuum coffee maker by Corning Glass Works.

PYREX VACUUM
COFFEE MAKER—REGENT

Size 8 Cup

PYREX VACUUM
COFFEE MAKER—AIKEN

Size 8 Cup

PYREX VACUUM COFFEE
MAKER—MANHATTAN

Size 8 Cup

PYREX VACUUM COFFEE
MAKER—COFFEE MISER

Size 4 Cup

Newer four and eight cup PYREX® coffee makers.

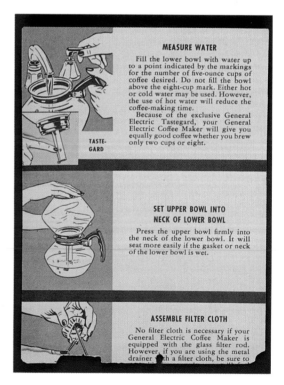

MEASURE WATER

Fill the lower bowl with water up to a point indicated by the markings for the number of five-ounce cups of coffee desired. Do not fill the bowl above the eight-cup mark. Either hot or cold water may be used. However, the use of hot water will reduce the coffee-making time.

Because of the exclusive General Electric Tastegard, your General Electric Coffee Maker will give you equally good coffee whether you brew only two cups or eight.

TASTE-GARD

**SET UPPER BOWL INTO
NECK OF LOWER BOWL**

Press the upper bowl firmly into the neck of the lower bowl. It will seat more easily if the gasket or neck of the lower bowl is wet.

ASSEMBLE FILTER CLOTH

No filter cloth is necessary if your General Electric Coffee Maker is equipped with the glass filter rod. However, if you are using the metal drainer with a filter cloth, be sure to

The first steps in preparing to use a vacuum coffee maker.

Two vacuum coffee makers with Bakelite handles. $125-150 each.

An electric vacuum coffee maker on its base. $125-150.

Two four cup and two eight cup vacuum coffee makers. $100-125 each.

Left: a coffee maker taken apart; *right:* the glass filter rod is in place and the coffee maker is assembled. $125-150 each complete unit.

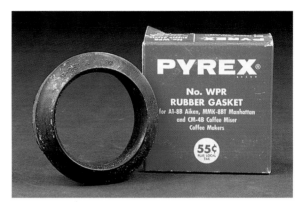

A rubber gasket used to seal the top and bottom bowls. $15-18 as packaged.

An unusual PYREX® vacuum coffee maker made in Japan. $50-65.

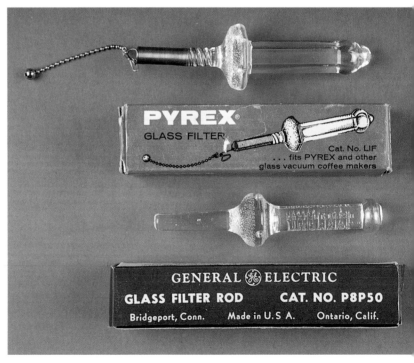

Glass filter rods and their original packaging. $15-18 as packaged.

Many companies utilized PYREX® parts in their own vacuum coffee makers. Several examples are shown.

The Universal Electric Crystal Coffee Maker. $125-150.

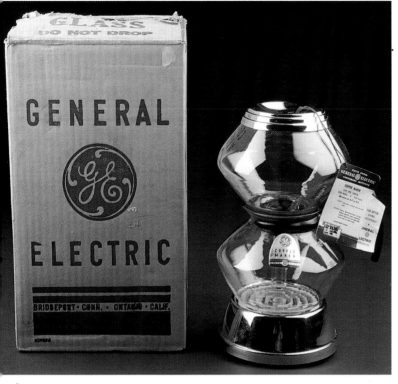

The General Electric Automatic Coffee Maker. $125-150.

The Cafex Glass Coffee Maker. $125-150.

Two General Electric Automatic Coffee Makers. $125-150 each.

"COFFEE AS YOU LIKE IT—AUTOMATICALLY"

Coffee flavored to your taste—that's what you'll get, every time, with the General Electric Automatic Coffee Maker. Here's all you do. Measure water in lower bowl with the convenient cup markings. Put one table-spoon* of coffee for each cup in up-per bowl. Press button, that's all! Coffee making's entirely automatic from then on. Heat turns on, water rises, heat cuts off automatically. Coffee flows into lower bowl, keeps piping hot as *low* heat turns on automatically. Clamp-on lid serves as table mat for inverted bowl.
*P.S. If you like a weaker brew, use less coffee per cup; stronger; use more.

Directions from General Electric on how to operate a coffee maker.

Three Ward coffee makers marked: "PYREX® BRAND GLASSWARE MADE IN U.S.A. FOR HILL SHAW CO." The one on the right has a four cup capacity, the other two are eight cup coffee makers. $100-125 each.

COFFEE MAKERS - SILEX

It would be remiss to ignore the PYREX® role in SILEX coffee making products. During the 1940s, many glass parts on SILEX coffee makers were marked with both the SILEX and PYREX® marks.

HOW TO PREPARE COFFEE

1. Fill lower bowl with water to a point two inches below top of neck. This gives the full capacity of your Silex. If you wish fewer cups you can make two cups less than the rated capacity. (In the two-cup size, you can make one cup.) To shorten the time of making coffee, use hot water. Hot water may be heated in the lower bowl directly over the flame of your range. A tea kettle is unnecessary.

2. Place one level tablespoonful of coffee per cup, and one extra "for the pot," in the upper bowl. This is the quantity that pleases most people. If you prefer stronger coffee, add a larger quantity to the upper bowl; if you wish weaker coffee, use a smaller quantity.

3. Place the lower bowl over the heat. Seat the upper bowl in the lower by giving it a slight twist to make an air-tight seal between upper and lower vessel.

4. In a few minutes the water in the lower bowl will rise and mix with the coffee in the upper bowl. A little water will always remain in the lower bowl. This is necessary to prevent heat breakage.

5. Stir the mixture in the upper bowl with a spoon.

6. Now that all the water has risen to the upper bowl, steam will commence rising through the tube to agitate the mixture in the upper bowl. At this time, if you are using the electric model, you should turn off the heat. Electric models are designed so that by keeping the glassware on the stove, the water and coffee are automatically held in contact the proper length of time.

If you are using a non-electric model upon a kitchen range, turn down the gas or move to a portion of the stove where the heat is less

intense. The water should remain in the upper bowl three to four minutes. Keep the Silex over low heat for two minutes, then turn off the heat. The water will then remain in the upper bowl about another minute, thus allowing the water to remain in contact with the ground coffee the proper time of three to four minutes.

7. As the lower bowl cools a vacuum is created, which draws the brew down into the lower bowl.

8. Remove the upper bowl.

9. Pour from lower bowl.

Washing Your Silex

Merely rinse both upper and lower bowls under running water. Hot water is preferable. If a small amount of brewed coffee is allowed to dry in the lower bowl, there may be a slight discoloration or stain. This can be removed with a strong solution of baking soda or soap. If the stain does not respond to a baking soda or soap solution, drop a small piece of cloth or coarse paper into the solution in the bowl and shake. This provides a scouring action that will serve to clean completely the inside of the lower bowl.

Remove entire spring and filter assembly by pulling chain at the bottom and releasing the hook. Hold filter under running water until all coffee is washed away. The cloth may be removed entirely for thorough cleaning with soap and water. The cloth must be kept clean. The cloth may be used repeatedly, as long as it remains sweet and soft. An extra filter cloth is furnished with your Silex. Additional cloth strainers can be purchased from Silex dealers. Use a new cloth whenever there is any doubt as to the cleanliness of the one in use. Never place a new filter cloth over an old one; remove the old one first.

Note: It is not necessary to put the cover on upper bowl while coffee is being made. Invert the cover on the table and use it as an utensil for holding bowl after it has been removed.

Directions For Using Tea Stopper
WHEN SERVING COFFEE

Many people use the stopper on the lower bowl when serving coffee. Simply "snap" the stopper into place in the neck of the lower bowl. It enhances the appearance of the lower bowl and helps keep your coffee warm over a longer period.

An explanation of how to use a vacuum coffee maker by the SILEX Company.

A 1941 advertisement.

Various SILEX models are offered in this advertisement.

A grouping of four SILEX coffee makers very similar to the advertisement. All share the same mark: "PYREX® BRAND GLASSWARE MADE IN U.S.A. FOR THE SILEX CO." *Two on left still with bases (stoves):* $125-150; *Two on right:* $100-125.

SILEX, as did Corning Glass Works, embellished the coffee makers in various designs.

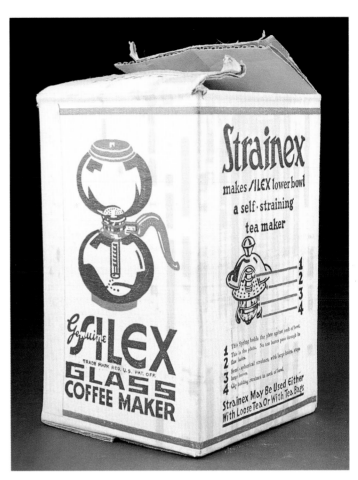

An original package for a SILEX coffee maker made with PYREX® glass. This vacuum coffee maker would convert into a tea maker by using a different lid on the lower bowl as shown on the side panel of the carton.

A SILEX coffee maker and a SILEX tea maker with the Strainex lids that were required to make tea. *Left:* $125-150; *right:* $35-45; lids in original packaging: $20-25 each.

A SILEX replacement part. $20-25 as packaged.

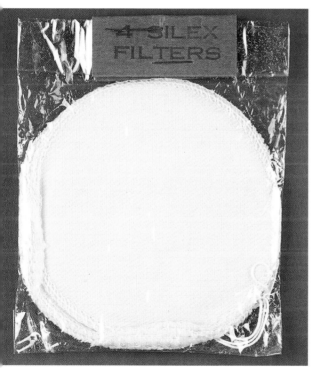

An unopened coffee filter. $10-12 as packaged.

A 3.25" coffee measure marked: "DRIPPEX TRADEMARK MEASURING CUP THE SILEX CO. HARTFORD CONN U.S.A." $10-12.

Marked "GENUINE SILEX," this vacuum coffee maker shares a PYREX® mark. $75-100.

8" and 11.25" CHEMEX Filter Coffee makers marked: "CHEMEX U.S. PATENT 2,411,340 MADE IN U.S.A. FROM PYREX® BRAND GLASS." $40-45 each.

A more recent (1960s?) CHEMEX Filter Coffee maker. $35-40.

COFFEE MAKERS - CHEMEX

A sleek, modern-looking design was available with the CHEMEX Filter-Coffee maker. Made from "one single piece of PYREX® glass," these offered a new look and method for tasting the ultimate in coffee. Using the special CHEMEX filter, coffee or tea filters down during preparation and then is served from a stunning carafe after reaching the bottom reservoir.

An older CHEMEX box.

COFFEE MAKERS –
A FEW OTHER UNIQUE EXAMPLES

Here is a final look at a few other, interesting ways to prepare coffee, plus one "extra." These items are all created with the advantage that PYREX® glass offers.

This Melitta coffee maker is 10.5" tall. The filtration system is plastic but the carafe is PYREX® glassware.

The Melior coffee maker is 8" tall. Both the handle and knob are made of Bakelite. The glass is marked with a PYREX® stamp.

Both electric coffee makers use PYREX® glass. The 12" tall avocado green Sunbeam coffee maker has increments for 4, 6, 8, 10, or 12 cups of brew. The 11.5" tall cream colored PROCTOR-SILEX coffee maker has a capacity of 12 cups but only has increments for 5, 7, 9, and 11 cups.

Although not a coffee maker, this diminutive Coffee Maker Barometer is worth noting. Styled like the Vacuum Coffee maker, this hand blown item will indicate changes in atmospheric pressure and thereby assist in weather prediction.

Left: 12" Sunbeam electric coffee percolator; *Right:* PROCTOR-SILEX coffee percolator. $25-30 each.

Melitta coffee maker. $35-40.

Melior coffee maker. $75-90.

SAUCEPANS & DOUBLE BOILERS

When FLAMEWARE was first marketed in 1936, saucepans with removable handles (holders) were produced before the advent of double boilers. As shown in the first advertisement, one handle could be utilized on any number of saucepans by simply snapping it on and off as necessary. The original handle style had a glass knob inside the metal loop. To remove the handle, one would depress this "button." This bit of glass was later removed from the handle to reduce production costs.

In 1943, an all-glass, removable handle became available. The glass was designed to resist heat during use. Although the saucepan or double boiler became hot, the glass handle was to remain cool. This glass handle was replaced first by an all-metal handle (the button-less handle mentioned above) and, eventually, by a permanent glass handle.

During World War II, a wooden handle was used. An advertisement from 1955 shows an non-removable all-glass handle was in use twelve years after the debut of the first glass handle design.

Coffee Maker Barometer and box. $35-40.

A "button-less" handle is being used in the FLAMEWARE advertisement.

The FLAMEWARE handles in this advertisement are permanently affixed.

Note the wooden handle on the saucepan on the left. This would
sell for $60-70; the others would cost less, $30-40.

One and one-and-a-half quart saucepans were the first sizes of FLAMEWARE cookware available. Lids and additional sizes were quickly added as public acceptance occurred. Double boilers also followed, the first being offered in 1937—also in one and one-and-a half quart sizes.

As with other PYREX® glassware, every attempt was made to satisfy the consumer. Minor design changes took place, including eventually moving the two handles of the double boiler closer together for easier lifting. The knobs on lids changed. Diameters changed, so bases and covers would mix and match. Even the design of the upper double boiler unit was altered so it could be used independently as a sauce pan. Every effort was made to keep American housewives delighted with the performance of their FLAMEWARE until this line's termination in 1979.

A saucepan with the original label and paper. $20-30 for saucepan;
add $5 for label and $5 for paper.

Two saucepans with covers. $30-40 each.

Two saucepans and covers with the "double boiler" shape. $40-50 each.

The two quart FLAMEWARE saucepan joins the 7" skillet, 1 quart, and 1.5 quart saucepans with an introductory price of $1.35 in September 1946.

FLAMEWARE sizes and prices are given in this mid-1940s advertisement.

Double boilers and the rarely-seen egg poacher. Double boilers, $75-85 each; egg poacher, $40-50.

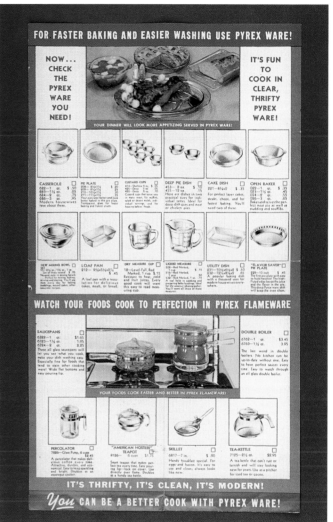

A double boiler is showcased in this PYREX® advertisement.

FLAMEWARE sizes and prices are included in this Corning brochure from the mid-1940s.

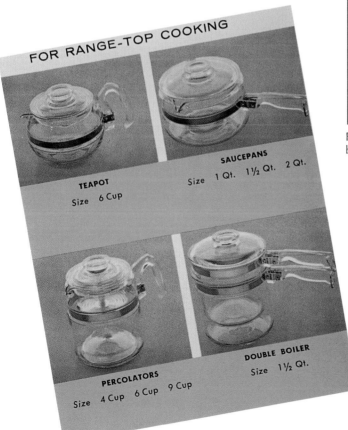

A saucepan and double boiler are featured in a PYREX® brochure.

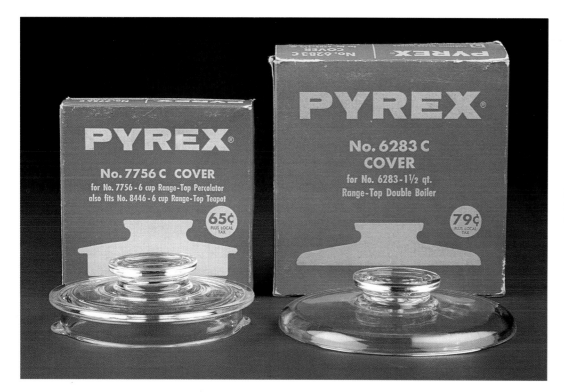

PYREX® replacement covers in the original boxes. $15-20 each as packaged.

SKILLETS

A seven-inch skillet with one handle was part of the original FLAMEWARE line. As shown in this catalogue page, one could cook and serve the meal in this handy item.

A skillet is shown in a 1945 catalogue. Note the glass "button" in the handle.

Three 7" skillets. $20-25 each.

In the late 1940s, an eight-inch two-handled skillet was introduced. A seven-inch skillet with two tab handles was later offered in 1952.

Two 7" skillets. Note the glass "buttons" in the handles. $20-25 each.

A boxed set of PYREX® FLAMEWARE. $85-100 as packaged.

A PYREX® advertisement includes a
one pint skillet for ninety cents.

The 7" skillet with holder is offered for $1.49.

TEAKETTLES

Introduced two years after FLAMEWARE production began, there was only one teakettle in this line. Unfortunately, there is no picture of one in this reference. It had a two-and-a-half quart capacity with an older style FLAMEWARE lid and retailed for $2.95. Because it had a wide-necked opening, this teakettle was also recommended for cooking vegetables, fruits, and soups, and was additionally suggested for use as a beverage server.

Contemporaries of PYREX® also made teakettles. A few of these competitors' kettles are presented here.

A tea-kettle with PYREX® glass, presumably sold by another manufacturer. $50-60 if glass survived in better, clearer condition. $20-25 as found.

A 10.75" GLASBAKE vacuum coffee maker and 7" tea-kettle made with PYREX® glass. Coffee maker, $70-100; tea-kettle, $75-85.

MAKE
A HANDY
TEA MAKER
OF YOUR
SILEX
LOWER BOWL

STRAINEX—60c Tea as well as coffee can be made with your Silex . . . and just as *strains as it pours* simply. In the lower bowl merely add tea to boiling water, then snap this Strainex into the neck, and pour. Not a leaf can pass through this ingenious device. It has two baffles — one to catch the large leaves, and one to stop the small ones. And if you use tea bags . . . the Strainex has a slot through which you can pull the string and lift the bag above the tea.

This bright little stopper, snapping into the neck of your Silex lower bowl, holds the heat within the bowl, keeps your coffee warm longer. It makes pouring easier. And if you use teabags . . . **STOPPER—50c** it makes your Silex a combination tea and coffee maker, for it has a slit through which you can draw the string to lift it above the brewed tea.

Buy from Your Dealer, or
THE SILEX COMPANY
Hartford, Conn.

PRINTED IN U. S. A.   FORM 6A

A SILEX brochure explains how their Strainex lid converts the bottom bowl of a vacuum coffee maker to a tea-kettle.

A SILEX Tea Maker box. The Strainex lid is featured on a side panel of the package.

This is a Tea Kettle replacement part. Note the ribbed design is the same shown on the Glasbake coffee maker and tea-kettle. This is compatible with the tea-kettle shown on page 191. $25-30. *Courtesy of Janice Johnston/Behind the Green Door*

A Spiegel's catalogue includes a tea-kettle for only $1.39.

TEAPOTS

The six-cup "American Hostess" FLAMEWARE teapot was first offered in 1943 and sold for $1.75. The advertisement reflected the patriotic mood of a country united in the efforts of World War II.

As long as FLAMEWARE production continued, this teapot remained available. The handle and cover underwent subtle changes, as was true for virtually all PYREX® products, and the price slowly increased. In the cookbook, *PYREX® Prize Recipes,* the following suggestion is offered: "A PYREX® teapot is fine for fruit juices, spaghetti sauce, soups, and tops for tea."

The FLAMEWARE teapot price has risen to $1.95.

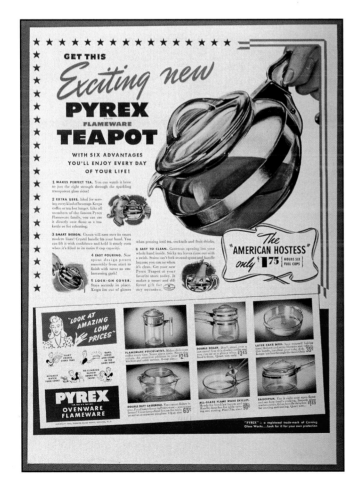

The "American Hostess" teapot is introduced at a price of $1.75, now $80-100.

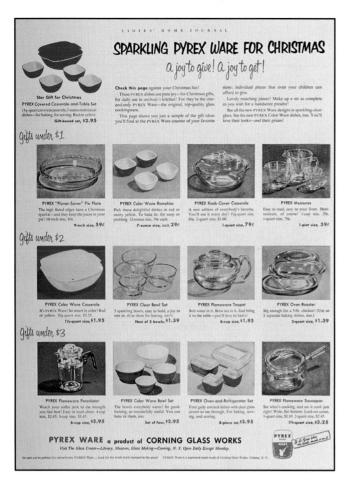

The teapot is part of a PYREX® Christmas advertisement.

A new handle design and a new price of $2.50 are shown in this advertisement, including a FLAMEWARE teapot.

A FINAL LOOK AT PYREX®
FLAMEWARE

Although there weren't a great many items made in FLAMEWARE, the offerings were extremely useful and continue to be among those most favored by PYREX® collectors. Just the fact that this line continued until 1979 speaks for its success.

Of all the items presented, the unusual coffee makers and complete double boilers are in the greatest demand at this time. However, this reference is missing a teapot and teakettle. In terms of availability in the contemporary marketplace, these items are quite rare, even if the demand for them is not quite as high.

CHAPTER THREE

PYREX® COLORS

Utilizing existing molds, PYREX® took on an entirely new look in 1947. World War II had ended and America was experiencing a new wave of prosperity. Babies were being born in record numbers. These expanding families, with growing incomes, needed to be fed; so, Corning Glass Works introduced a new generation of products—in bright colors, truly glass for living.

This new line of kitchen glass was the end result of the development of strong, durable dinnerware for use by the military during World War II. Advertisements not only emphasized the beauty, but also the strength of PYREX®.

To create this line of glassware, additional steps occurred. Color had to be sprayed onto white ("Opal") glass toward the final steps of manufacture. Patterns on the glassware meant there was an extra printing step. "Desert Dawn" bakeware was introduced in 1955. Made in "warm Desert Pink" and "gay Desert Yellow," these items had grey speckles mixed in the colors. Even though there weren't many different sizes and shapes of glassware made in PYREX® colors, all of these procedures created an entirely

new look. It was the multitude of colors and printed embellishments that resulted in so many varieties. Colors reflected the fashions of the time. As decorators advocated specific looks and styles, PYREX® kitchen glass followed suit, leaving a legacy of designs, colors, and combinations that document American tastes for almost thirty years.

This chapter reveals not only the rainbow palette of PYREX®, but other interesting kitchen, home, and glassware items from the late 1940s through the late 1960s. PYREX® had now become an important part of many products, often with other manufacturers' names on the items. Corning technology had become necessary to the military, had become an integral part of scientific work and research, was depended upon in construction for everything from glass to insulation, provided the world with containers, and on and on.

PYREX® celebrated seventy-five years of bringing quality glassware to America and the world in 1990. Who knows what fabulous Corning creations are yet to come in this new millennium!

The "Three Piece Seventy-fifth Anniversary Set" of PYREX®. Complete as shown with box and labels, $50-65.

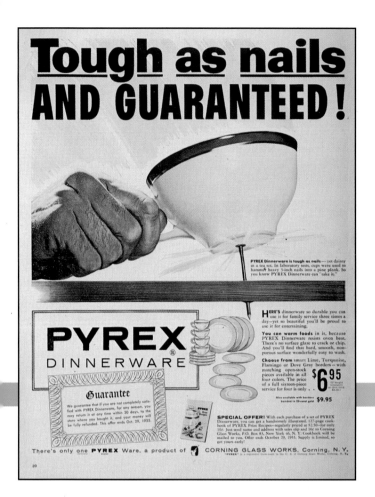
BANKS

The piggy bank was intended for personal use while the glass block bank was also a promotional piece. The 4.5" long pig is actually marked "PIGGY BANK" on each side, certainly enlightening anyone in doubt of his purpose. The 3.25" x 3.25" x 1.75" glass block from circa 1936 reads: "SAVE WITH PITTSBURGH PC CORNING GLASS BLOCKS."

Piggy bank, $100-125; Glass block bank, $35- $40.

BLENDERS

Both of these Waring blenders have PYREX® reservoirs. The white unit is 15" tall and the chrome model is 15.5" high. Renewed interest in barware makes these particularly desirable.

Waring blenders, $80-100 each.

BOTTLES

The 10.5" metal water bottle is from the St. Regis Hotel. There is a PYREX® glass liner inside to help insulate the cool water.

This plain, unassuming bottle is actually an insulin bottle measuring a mere 2.25". It is marked PYREX® on the bottom.

Juice bottles are listed in this chapter under "Carafes."

Insulin bottle, $10-12.

St. Regis water bottle, $50-60.

BOWLS

The first colored bowl set offered continues to be the most recognizable grouping, and therefore the most popular set of all. The famous "400 Multicolored Mixing Bowl" set has become known today as "Primary Mixing Bowls" or "Primary-colored Mixing Bowls." Each bowl is numbered and sized on the bottom. From largest to smallest they are: yellow, #404, 4 quarts, 10" diameter; green: #403, 2.5 quarts, 8.5" diameter; red, #402, 1.25 quarts, 7" diameter; and blue, #401, 0.5 quart, 5.5" diameter. The sizes and four digit numeration (404, 403, 302, 401) are consistent with all round PYREX mixing bowls. Newer "Primary Mixing Bowls" are a bit thinner than the original pieces of the 1940s. This subtle nuance does not effect value or collector enthusiasm.

The 400 Multicolored Mixing Bowl Set was offered for $2.50. It is the first colored PYREX® to be offered for sale with Ovenware and FLAMEWARE.

An original label remains on a Colored Bowl Set. Prices for sets in good condition seem to vary greatly throughout the country, with much higher prices in the South and on the West Coast than the Midwest and East. $70-120 per set of four.

NEW PYREX WARE PRICES

CASSEROLES
Round Utility Cover
682 — 1 qt. ....$ .69
683 — 1½ qt. .... .79
684 — 2 qt. .... .89
686 — 3 qt. 1.19

ROUND UTILITY DISHES
*453 — 8 oz. ....$ .10
*455 — 12 oz. .... .15

CASSEROLES
Round Knob Cover
623 — 1½ qt. ....$ .79
624 — 2 qt. .... .89
626 — 3 qt. 1.19

"FLAVOR-SAVER"
PIE PLATE
229 — 10" ....$ .59

PIE PLATES
208 — 8½" x 1½" ...$ .29
209 — 9½" x 1½" ... .35
210 — 10½" x 1½" ... .39

BOWL SET
95 — Set of three
   nested $1.19
2½ qt., 1½ qt., 1 qt.

UTILITY DISHES
231 — 10½x6½x2" ...$ .59
232 — 12⅜x8½x2" ... .79

CUSTARD
462 — 5 o
463 — 6½

COLOR BOWL SET
400 — Set of four
   nested $2.95
4 qt. 10" yellow, 2½ qt.
8½" green, 1¼ qt. 7" red,
½ qt. 5½" blue.

CAKE DISH
221 — 8⅜x2" ....$ .49

RED MARKED
MEASURING CUP
516 — One pint liquid $.50

4-PIECE FLAMEWARE
"GIFT SET"
*265 — Per set $2.45
Interchangeable handle—
Fits all three dishes.

SAUCEPANS
*6832 — 1 qt. $1.10
*6833 — 1½ qt. 1.25
*6834 — 2 qt. 1.35
*6817 — 7" Skillet .. .90

LOAF PANS
212 — 9⅛x5⅛x2⅞" ...$ .59
214 — 10⅜x5⅝x3⅜" .. .79

OTHER PYREX WARE
DISHES shown on
last three pages

SEE THE PYREX WARE DISHES ON DISPLAY
YOUR DEALER'S STORE
s PYREX Ware Replacement Parts.

The 400 bowls rose in price to $2.95
shortly after the set was introduced.

Within two years, the large four quart bowl was also available in red which, along with the four quart yellow bowl, could be purchased separately. Prices began to climb ever so slightly.

The "Opal Bowl Set" was produced only in 1954. As the period of manufacture was so brief, this totally white nest of bowls is an extremely rare set. The measurements are identical to the 400 set.

Ever eager to provide consumers with the latest in style, the 400 bowls were issued in colors that reflected the times. Turquoise, pink, and yellow sets were available in 1956.

The "Opal Bowl Set" with an original sticker. $100-120 per set of four.

Four turquoise bowls. $80-120 per set of four.

Shown is the largest four quart bowl in pink, which is the hardest of the four to find. Although this was sold as a set of four, one will rarely find more that the three smaller bowls. $100-120 per set of four.

Four yellow bowls. $80-120 per set of four.

The 300 bowls were introduced in 1957, having only three bowls: 8.5", 7", and 5.5".

With the advent of three bowl sets, colors and combinations abounded in both three and four bowl groupings. A sampling of the many varieties follows. As the popularity of certain colors and themes came and went, the interest collectors gave to specific designs changed. Early American themes and the 1960s shades of green, gold, and orange were popular in their day, but are in low demand at this time. The original colors, the 1950s colors (of turquoise, pink, and yellow), polkadots, and stripes are current favorites. Prices listed reflect collectors' demands at this time.

A 300 series nest of turquoise bowls is featured in this PYREX®brochure. These bowls sell for about $80-120 per set, while the matching Cinderella Casseroles in turquoise and pink are valued at $20-30 each. Cinderella bowls in pink are of the highest value at $60-75 set. Turquoise bowls have a slightly less value at $55-75 while Sandalwood remains in low demand. Oven and Freezer pieces (often referred to as "Refrigerator Dishes") are worth $25 per item in turquoise and in pink, whether solid or multicolored.

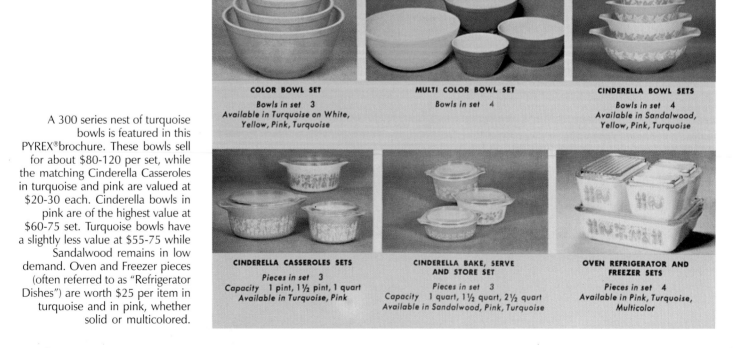

COLOR BOWL SET
Bowls in set 3
Available in Turquoise on White, Yellow, Pink, Turquoise

MULTI COLOR BOWL SET
Bowls in set 4

CINDERELLA BOWL SETS
Bowls in set 4
Available in Sandalwood, Yellow, Pink, Turquoise

CINDERELLA CASSEROLES SETS
Pieces in set 3
Capacity 1 pint, 1½ pint, 1 quart
Available in Turquoise, Pink

CINDERELLA BAKE, SERVE AND STORE SET
Pieces in set 3
Capacity 1 quart, 1½ quart, 2½ quart
Available in Sandalwood, Pink, Turquoise

OVEN REFRIGERATOR AND FREEZER SETS
Pieces in set 4
Available in Pink, Turquoise, Multicolor

Four bowls. $70-120 per set of four.

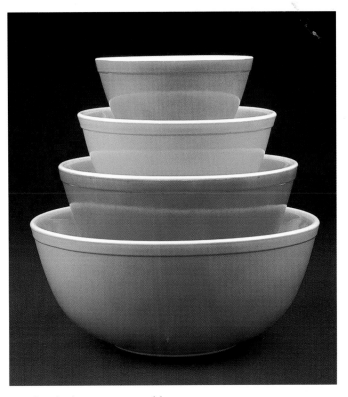

Four bowls. $50-75 per set of four.

"Verde." $50-75 per set of four.

Four "New Dot" bowls. Originally a set of three issued in 1967, the largest bowl, which has the greatest value, was added in 1969. Not pictured is the New Dot bowl in yellow The integrity of the dots is very important when assigning values. These bowls are worth about $20-25 each, with the exception of the green bowl, valued at $85-90.

Three "Early American" bowls introduced in 1961. $20-30 per set of three.

Similar colors to the previous bowls. $5-7 per bowl.

"Federal Eagle." $5-7 per bowl.

Colors from the 1960s. $8-10 per bowl.

"Crazy Daisy" motif from the 1960s. $5-7 per bowl.

"Spring Blossom Green" motif from the 1960s. $8-10 per bowl.

Colors from the 1960s. Left, "Woodland"; right, "Old Orchard." $8-10 per bowl.

Four "Americana" bowls introduced in 1966. $50-60 per set of four.

"Rainbow Stripes" bowls from 1965. Not shown is the least popular tan striped bowl. Prices per bowl, tan: $12-15; blue and yellow: $18-20; pink: $25-30.

Three "Americana" bowls in more popular colors. $45-55 per set of three.

Three "Butterprint" bowls introduced in 1959 when turquoise was a trendy color. $50-60 per set of three.

Cinderella bowls were introduced in 1958 and are easily recognizable by the two pour spout handles of different sizes. They were also produced with many colorful designs. These attributes made them a bright, if not whimsical, alternative to batter bowls, while being usable for baking, serving, and storing as well.

The shape was adapted and transformed into a line of casseroles with similar handles having matching colors and designs. As these were first issued in the late 1950s, the colors predominantly reflect those of the 1960s.

Four "Butterprint" Cinderella Bowls. $55-75 per set of four.

A brochure featuring the turquoise "Butterprint" Cinderella bowls.

Four "Gooseberry" Cinderella Bowls. $50-60 per set of four.

Another color scheme with the "Gooseberry" design. $12-15 per bowl.

Four Cinderella Bowls. "Daisy." $50-60 per set of four.

"Spring Blossom Green." Cinderella Bowls. $35-45 per set of four.

Two different Cinderella Bowls with 1960s florals. Back, "Crazy Daisy"; front, "Spring Blossom Green." $8-10 per bowl.

A grape vine pattern on a Cinderella bowl. $10-12 per bowl.

An incomplete set of "Early American" Cinderella bowls. $8-10 per bowl.

s WHY a dish worth its salt
PYREX® Ware
ake it even better

win praises galore from the family, guests, from s and neighbors when they taste the dishes you cook EX Ware. In fact, you'll even give yourself a medal as scover how much **easier** you can mix, bake, cook, freeze, and store.

re on your way with PYREX® WARE

rous glass keeps odors and flavors in the food in- of the utensil. "See-through" glass covers let you n-the-pot-boil" as you cook . . . Glass is easier to clean asier to keep clean) than metal cooking utensils. ause glass absorbs radiant heat, instead of reflecting n dishes bake faster. You even save gas or electricity, se cooking in glass means oven temperatures are lower.

here's HOW to make the most of cookin with PYREX® Ware

You can make everything from a main cours the coffee and cake for dessert in PYREX Wa aren't used to cooking in glass, a few hints practice will help you make best use of this rial. For instance, the Heat Spreader Grid PYREX Brand Range-top Ware) should be us an electric range for surface cooking . . . and the temperature at LOW or MEDIUM. (If food merely reduce heat.) Always place food, fa utensil before placing it over direct heat. D for deep-fat frying.

PYREX Ware is versatile. You can cook, ba and store your favorite dishes . . . and they than ever before. And the more you use it, th enjoy using PYREX Ware!

here's the VARIETY that makes PYREX® so popular with so many people in so ma

From the formal-gourmet host to the casua hostess . . . in professional kitchens, in hote restaurants—everywhere, every day, more pe ing to glass for cookery at its best. Here ar more popular PYREX Brand items. See you complete selection and prices.

A brochure for "Early American" PYREX®.

Two "Balloon" Cinderella bowls sold as a "Chip and Dip Set." Several different patterns were used to create these sets. $20-25.

Four Cinderella Gooseberry mixing bowls. Complete set $60-75.

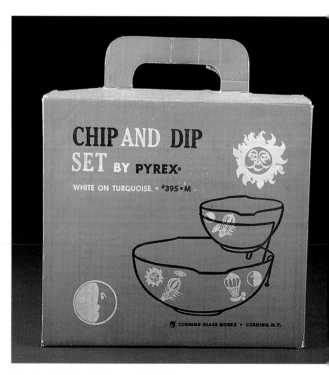

The box for the "Chip and Dip."

A PYREX® brochure exhibits the "terra" options.

"terra's" beauty on display.

The "terra" pattern was issued in 1964. Bowls, plates, casseroles, and mugs (having no handles) comprised this earthy pattern. Although not particularly popular when introduced, "terra" is now starting to get noticed.

The next grouping of bowls, introduced in 1949, could also be presented in this chapter in the casserole section. Covered, the large bowls become "Hostess" casseroles, but uncovered they are ramekins. The smaller bowls had no covers and were listed in catalogues as ramekins. The advertisement shows two different sets having differently-sized pieces, each being offered at $2.95. Note that one large bowl includes a cover and the other does not.

Just as PYREX® was manufacturing clear Ovenware and FLAMEWARE for other companies, this was also true with "Opal" glass. These bowls were produced for Hamilton Beach electric mixers.

Very much in demand are the Delphite mixing bowls, which sell for about $25-35 per bowl. Delphite PYREX® is also shown as a divided dish and with the refrigerator dishes in this chapter.

A "terra" grouping including 300 bowls. Bowls and mugs $10-12 each.

A variety of sizes and combinations of "Hostess Sets" in an advertisement from 1949.

This five piece "Oven-and-Table" set never had a lid. The larger bowl is 2.5 quarts and the smaller ones are each 12 ounces. This was the standard for "Oven-and-Table" sets. Without a box or labels in yellow, blue, turquoise, rose, black, or red, large bowl: $15-20; small bowls in yellow, blue, turquoise, or red: $10-15 each. Set as boxed: $75-85.

A lid changed the turquoise, red, or yellow 2.5 quart and 1.5 quart bowls to casseroles. Either size large bowl: $15-20; lid: $10-15; small bowls (ramekins) $10-15 each.

Three "Opal" glass bowls for electric mixers. $8-10 each. Add $5.00 for the original label.

Delphite PYREX® was manu-
factured in Canada. These
"Bluebelle" bowls are among
the most difficult to find and
remain extremely popular.
$25-35 per bowl.

CAKE DISHES

Cake dishes were also referred to as "round baking and serving dishes." The message to the homemaker was to not merely relegate your colored cake dish for baking cakes. One could bake *any* item and bring it to the table as the bright, decorator colors would surely enhance the table setting. Cake dishes are usually found in the 1950s colors of Flamingo, a deep hue of pink, and Lime. Although marked "8 INCH" on the bottom, these dishes actually measure 10" handle-to-handle. Note how a PYREX® lid will fit over the piece, adding to the usefulness of the cake dish.

2 cake dishes. $15-18 each; lid, $5-7.

CANISTERS

Canisters joined the PYREX® line in the 1950s. The Cracker Barrel and The Cookie Jar were among the earliest offerings. Later additions coordinated with other PYREX® glassware. The lids either mimicked motifs already being used or they matched colors used elsewhere.

Shown in 1960s colors, these canisters have PYREX® marks printed near their bottoms. "Spice of Life" (floral motif) canister: 4" tall, 6.25" diameter, $10-12; green-lidded canister: 3.75" tall, 4.75" diameter, $8-10.

SALT AND PEPPER SHAKER SET

Size 4¼"
Available in 0, 2, 18, 19

CRACKER BARREL

Capacity
1 pound of Crackers

The one pound Cracker Barrel is part of a brochure from the late 1950s. The shakers shown on top are $8-10 a pair. Add $5 for original packaging.

The Cracker Barrel is paired with The Cookie Jar. Both are 7" tall with a 6" opening and marked: "PYREX® MADE IN U.S.A." $15-18 each.

A 10" and 8.75" carafe, each with plastic lids. $10-12 each.

CARAFES

Many carafe sizes, shapes, and styles were marketed. Some were specifically designed for storing and serving chilled beverages such as juice, while others were meant for hot liquids such as coffee. With a fruit design printed on a carafe, it would suggest to the consumer that the manufacturer certainly intended it for juices. However, PYREX® glassware is durable and resistant to temperatures, whether cool or hot, so often carafes could be used as the homemaker chose. The first photographs suggest carafes intended to serve juices and other cold drinks.

The carafe with the cork stopper is quite unique and very intriguing. It is specifically marked, "CAUTION - FOR COLD LIQUIDS ONLY." It is ten inches tall and marked both "1 QT 1 L"—one quart and one liter.

Six carafes ranging in heights from 8" - 9.5". $12-18 each.

Salt and pepper shakers match this 10" carafe. Carafe, $10-12; shakers, $8-10 per pair.

Turquoise diamonds remind one of the 1950s. The carafe is 9.5" with increments to 48 ounces and the matching tumblers are 3.5". Carafe, $12-18; tumblers, $4-5 each. Expect to pay more if purchasing this together as a set.

These carafes seem destined for java, and some even came with their own warming tray. Again, the sizes, shapes, and styles are numerous.

Carafe with cork stopper. $30-40.

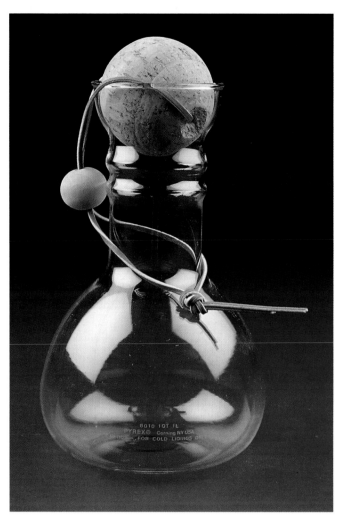

This 1950s PYREX® carafe came with a candle warmer. $30-35 if originally boxed as shown.

A 1950s brochure presents the modern ways a modern homemaker can serve a warm cup of coffee.

FOR COFFEE AND BEVERAGE SERVING

PYREX JUICE SERVER BOTTLE
Size 1 Qt. 1½ Qt.

PYREX LITTLE GOLD JUG
Size 2 Cup

PYREX MAGIC CRADLE
Adjusts itself to fit most Pyrex Casseroles
Perfect for table serving

PYREX CARAFES
with or without Candle Warmer
Size 8 cup and 12 cup

CINDERELLA CARAFE
with Candle Warmer
Size 8 cup and 12 cup

DELUXE CARAFE with
Electric Warming Tray and Cord
Size 12 Cup

PYREX carafe with candle warmer 8 cup capacity #288. This originally sold for $2.88. As shown with box $30-35. *Courtesy of Janice Johnston/ Behind the Green Door*

A carafe and electric warming tray from the 1950s. Carafe, $15-20; tray, $25-30.

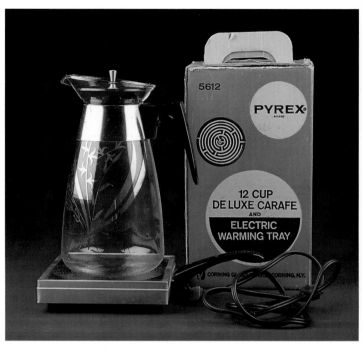

A carafe and electric warming tray from the 1950s. Carafe, $15-20; tray, $25-30; add $15 for the box.

Five carafes ranging in size from 7.25" - 9.75". The Melitta carafe (front right) is marked: "CORNING-BRAND HEAT-PROOF GLASS." The carafe in the back right is marked: "PYREX® BRAND LCR-12 MADE IN USA FOR THE SILEX CO." The other three have the same mark: "PYREX® MADE IN USA." $15-20 each.

All three carafes have aluminum handles and measure between 9" - 9.75". The one on the left is the only one still retaining a mark. $15-20 each.

Plastic handles are on all five carafes measuring from 9" - 9.5" The carafe in the front left is the same as the two in the back but has turquoise flowers and 2, 4, and 6 cup increments. The front center carafe is marked: "PYREX® BRAND GLASSWARE MADE IN USA FOR THE SILEX COMPANY." $15-20 each.

These carafes have wire handles. The 10" and 6.75" carafes on the left are the same style and are marked: "PYREX® BRAND GLASSWARE MADE IN USA FOR WEICO." The 9.75" carafe in the back right has no mark. The carafe in the front right is 10" tall and marked: "PYREX® BRAND GLASSWARE MADE IN U.S.A. BEVERAGE SERVER." $15-20 each.

Three single-serve carafes are marked, "PYREX® BRAND GLASSWARE MADE IN THE U.S.A. FOR THE SILEX CO." $10-12 each.

This advertising carafe set is actually not uncommon. $40-50 as boxed.

CASSEROLES

Versatility and variety best characterize the casseroles being manufactured during this period of time of the late 1940s through the late 1960s. Although there were only a few basic sizes and shapes, the surface treatments give the illusion of almost infinite possibilities.

This page from a PYREX® brochure shows many of the basic colored casseroles and the lid options.

Lids were made with and without knobs. Some lids were smooth and others, particularly those of the Space Saver Casserole, had ridges. Lids were produced in clear glass, colored glass, clear glass with printed designs, and "Opal" glass with designs. A sampling of

lid styles is shown, but countless other combinations exist, some as one-of-a kind offerings for specific bottoms. Lids without knobs were also designed to serve as trivets or tiles to protect surfaces from the hot contents in the casserole.

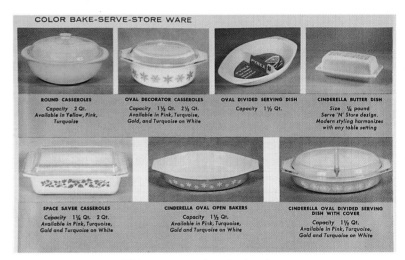

Many casseroles and lids are pictured in this brochure.

Cake dishes (see page 116) and Casseroles were boxed together with a single lid that was compatible for both. These sets were only available in Flamingo, although separately these items were marketed in other colors.

DECO Casserole which should have a black plastic underplate, if complete. $125-150, as shown $100.

123

3 oval lids with printed designs. $5-7 each.

2 "Opal" lids with designs, and one fired-on lid in brown. $5-7 each.

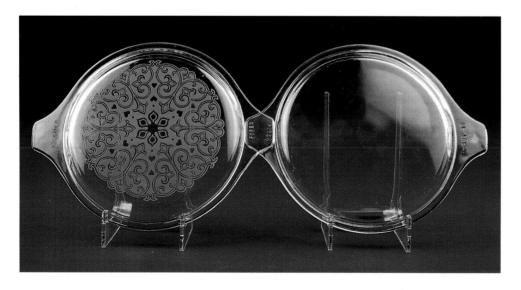

A printed and a plain round lid. $5-7 each.

A brochure showcases the complete "Daisy" line.

Many casseroles were briefly offered as promotional items. They were made available seasonally, for the Christmas holidays, for example. Other casseroles were part of named collections, allowing one to saturate a kitchen in lovely matching PYREX® colors.

Yellow was a strong decorator color in the 1950s and 1960s. The "Daisy" line was created to satisfy the need for matching yellow bakeware. However, other yellow pieces were available, both plain and with printed designs. Yellow is beginning to enjoy a resurgence of interest today.

Another important color was pink, particularly in the 1950s. A variety of embellishments were used to create a diverse selection. Whether pink on white or white on pink, PYREX® with pink is perhaps the most sought-after bakeware at this time.

Five "Daisy" pieces. $20-30 each.

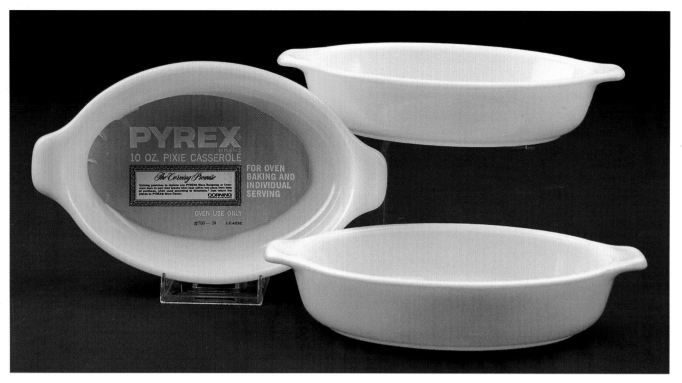

These shades of yellow would blend with "Daisy" casseroles or stand alone. $10-12 each. Add $5 for an original label.

1.5 quart casserole with matching lid. $20-25.

2.5 quart casserole. $20-25.

2 quart round casserole. $18-20.

Three Space Saver casseroles/ freezer server dishes. *Front left*: Scroll design introduced in 1958, *back*: 2 quart Turquoise Cinderella serving casserole from 1960,
front right: a different "Daisy" design begun in 1957. $20-25 each, add $5-7 for a
cradle.

Turquoise was a strong 1950s color, and a 1950s brochure shows a complete set of turquoise PYREX®. Note that this collection was also available in today's very popular pink and the less important gold on ivory. Other shades of blue followed turquoise, with blue on white and white on blue. Once again a relatively popular color, blue is very collectible. What was made in turquoise and blue was also made in many other colors, with various surface embellishments. Pinks, blues, and yellows are currently the most popular colors, while browns, greens, and golds get little attention.

Three one quart covered casseroles. *Left*: "Snowflake" probably 1960s; *middle*: "Butterprint" introduced in 1959; *right*: rare advertising item probably early 1960s. $20-22 each.

Now make your set complete with matching colors. Most pieces are also available in Pink and Gold on Ivory.

1.5 pint covered casseroles. *Left*: "Snowflake" probably 1960s; *right*: "Blue Stripe" introduced in 1966. $20-22 each.

A 1950s brochure shows turquoise bakeware. Today any of these items in pink would sell for about 25% more, and ivory with gold for about 50% less.

1.5 quart "Bluebird" casserole from 1959, complete with cradle and box. Casserole $18-20; cradle $5-7; box $10-15.

Three 1.5 quart covered casseroles. "Snowflake" is probably from the 1960s, the "Butterfly Gold" floral is a 1960s color and the "Butterprint" design was introduced in 1959. $20-22 each.

Three 1.5 quart covered casseroles. White "Snowflake" on black (actually called Charcoal) began in 1957, as did the turquoise "Snowflake." Today Charcoal in good condition is difficult to find. The garland is probably from the 1960s. $20-22 each.

Four 2.5 quart covered casseroles. Left to right, 1961 design made in Canada (also made in white with gold); "Colonial Brown" design probably from the 1960s; "Zodiac" design from 1961; a tree-of-life type of design, probably from the 1950s. $18-20 each.

2 quart casseroles were available with futuristic candle warmers in 1956, creating a "Jetson-like" appearance that is very popular today. The value in these items is truly in the complete set, not just the glass. Note the three different lid treatments. Casserole bottoms, $10-15 each; glass lids, $5 each; metal lids, $10-12 each; candle warmer, $15-20 each.

Early American colors and themes that were quite popular in the 1960s are no longer in demand. Many collectors do not seek kitchen glass evoking this look.

1.5 quart, 1 quart, and 1 pint casseroles clearly show the "Cinderella" handles. One handle is a bit larger than the other, presumably making holding and pouring easier to coordinate. $8-10 each.

PYREX® that survived with the original package would normally be in demand. This pattern is not particularly popular, so still having the box minimally affects its value. As shown, $35-40. Covered casseroles would sell for about $8-10 each.

The "Gold Acorn" design from 1960 is also being overlooked by many collectors. Shown also are "Early American" and "Spring Blossom Green." $8-10 each.

The use of color and enhancements continued into the 1960s. A sampling of these items is provided.

Two 8 ounce individual covered casseroles in Lime and Flamingo. $7-10 each.

Two 1 quart covered casseroles. $12-18 each.

The cradle for the 2.5 quart charcoal covered casserole is quite uncommon, $45-50. 1.5 pint covered casserole in gold with a fruit design, $15-18.

Golden Scroll was created with 24 carat gold and should not be used in a microwave oven. This 1959 design was also available in a Chip and Dip set made from two "Cinderella bowls." $18-20.

2.5 quart shallow casserole and cover in "Golden Honeysuckle" from 1963. $15-18.

Two "Cinderella Space Saver" covered casseroles. *Left*: a 1961 design $15-18 ; *right*: a 1958 design popular today due to the rooster theme, $20-25; add $5 for a cradle.

2.5 quart "Medallion" covered casserole from 1962. This design is not particularly popular so having the box minimally affects the value. $18-20.

1.5 quart "Town and Country" covered casserole from 1964. This design is not particularly popular so having the box minimally affects the value. "Town and Country" was produced in several color combinations. $18-20.

"Cinderella Buffet Twins" from 1959. This design is not particularly popular, so having the box minimally affects the value; however, dual casseroles are quite uncommon. $30-35.

Cradles were very much a part of PYREX® casseroles. They were made from wood, metal, and a combination of both. As many casseroles were promotional items, they were sold with specific cradles. Always putting the consumer first, PYREX® introduced the "Magic Cradle" in 1961. It extends from 12.5" to 16", allowing it to fit almost every PYREX® casserole made.

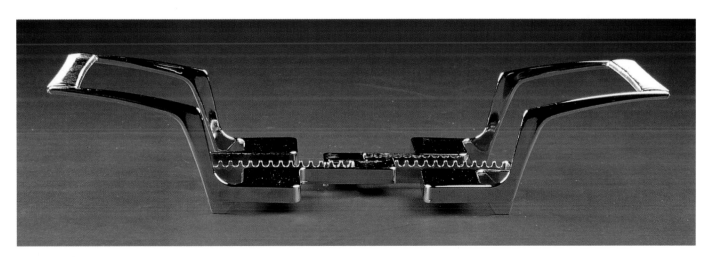

The "Magic Cradle." $12-15.

A brochure for the "Magic Cradle."

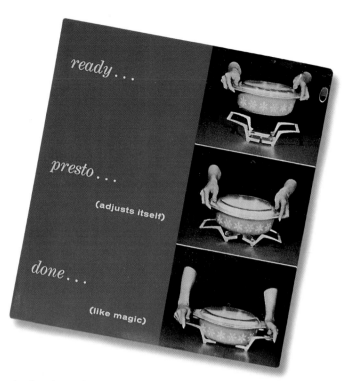

The brochure demonstrates the ease in using the "Magic Cradle."

CHRISTMAS DECORATIONS

PYREX® glassware had become a part of business, industry, and domestic life. How better to demonstrate the complete nature of PYREX® in all aspects of American life than with these Christmas tree ornaments?

Ornaments $1 each, add $3 for the box.

CUSTARD CUPS

Five fired-on custard cups which were made in Canada. These are 3.5" in diameter and 2.25" deep. $12-15 each.

DINNERWARE

In the late 1930s and early 1940s, Macbeth-Evans Division of Corning Glass Works produced a line of tableware called Cremax. Given fired-on rims, it was sold as "Bordette" in dark colors and "Rainbow" in pastel colors. The Windsor design on Cremax is also known as the Depression Glass pattern "Chinex Classic," recognized particularly for the castle design on blue-trimmed dinnerware. Delphite Cremax was made in Canada under the PYREX® brand. It is quite popular with today's collectors. For more information on these patterns, read *Mauzy's Depression Glass, Third Edition.*

A "Rainbow" grouping. No pricing is provided, as one can usually find these items for extremely reasonable amounts at flea markets and second hand shops.

A "Chinex Classic" grouping.

9" Cremax vegetable bowl in Delphite. $16.

PYREX® dinnerware, a new line introduced after World War II, is extremely durable. Much of this dinnerware has survived, finding its way to the antique marketplace. Initially offered in Dove Gray, Turquoise, Lime, and Flamingo, this dinnerware could be purchased with or without 22 carat gold trim. A starting service of sixteen pieces was only $5.95.

A Cremax label.

A slightly different shade of blue in a Cremax sugar bowl. $10.

This advertisement shows the four original colors of PYREX® dinnerware.

Two additional colors are now available, and the price has increased as shown in this advertisement.

Regency Green (the most difficult color to locate today) and Royal Burgundy were later added and were also available with or without the gold trim. Prices had now risen to $6.95 for sixteen pieces, but a free Cupboard Storage Rack was included.

Collectors are just noticing PYREX® dinnerware and the demand is beginning to increase. For those seeking to create a truly vintage kitchen, it will contribute nicely. Bowls and serving pieces are the most difficult items to locate. Certainly the condition of the colored band is crucial in determining value. As always, items with a gold trim can not go in a microwave oven!

A brochure pictures the basic place setting. Four of these groupings comprised one starting service of sixteen pieces.

Flamingo dinnerware. *Back row*: 9" bowl, 8.25" plate, 10" plate; *front row*: 6.25" bowl, cup and saucer. No pricing is provided, as one can usually find these items for extremely reasonable amounts at flea markets and second hand shops.

Lime dinnerware. 10" plate, 8.25" plate, cup and saucer, 9" bowl with gold trim.

Turquoise 10" and 8.25" plate and Dove Gray cup and saucer.

The popularity of PYREX dinnerware has significantly grown since the publication of the first edition of this book. In response to readers' requests a value listing is now included to provide reasonable guidance in what one can expect to see price-wise in the marketplace. When utilizing this reference keep in mind the following factors:

1. Condition, condition, condition. Look for brightly colored borders.

2. Gold trim does not make an item more valuable, this is a matter of personal taste.

3. The four pieces in the starting set are the most common pieces. Serving pieces, creamers, and sugars are much more difficult to locate.

Item	Flamingo, Turquoise, Dove Gray	Royal Burgundy, Regency Green,	Lime
Bowl, 6.25" soup or cereal	$8.00	$12.00	$5.00
Bowl, 9" serving	$15.00	$25.00	$10.00
Creamer	$10.00	$15.00	$8.00
Cup	$5.00	$8.00	$3.00
Plate, 8.25"	$8.00	$12.00	$5.00
Plate, 10"	$8.00	$14.00	$5.00
Saucer	$3.00	$4.00	$2.00
Sugar bowl	$10.00	$15.00	$8.00

Two 5.5" cereal bowls.

PYREX Restaurantware is becoming more abundant in antiques and collectibles markets. Once again, condition is the primary concern. Glassware is currently selling for a few dollars apiece. Many designs are quite institutional with minimal use of colors. However, careful hunting will reward you with trims in vivid red and even purple! Expect to pay more for colorful and intricate designs.

7.5" plate, 9" plate, 6.75" plate, two 5.5" plates.

PYREX® was also made for children. These divided plates with matching mugs are in great demand. An extra tab of glass seen near the bottom of the plate, was placed there to allow for stable stacking of these dishes.

Child's plate, $30-40 each; child's mug, $25-30. Not pictured is the cereal bowl, $30-40.

PYREX® WARE Toy Plastic Replica "Play-Set," $75-100.

While visiting children's dishes, it is worth noting a "Play-Set" made in plastic. This PYREX® set includes miniature refrigerator dishes, a FLAMEWARE percolator, and a 300 bowl set.

Later additions in PYREX® dinnerware include Corelle livingware. These patterns were quite complete, having dinnerware, serving pieces, and accessories. Although the dinnerware is not particularly collectible at this time, certain accessories are starting to gain favor, particularly butter dishes. Dating from the early 1960s, these "Cinderella butter dishes" sold for $1.49 each. As some were made in the same designs as particular casseroles and bowls, they are appropriate companion pieces.

All three of these butter dishes have matching bowls, casseroles, and refrigerator dishes. Top to bottom, "Butterfly Gold," "Butterprint," "Spring Blossom Green." $12-15 each.

DIVIDED DISHES

The "Cinderella Oval Divided Serving Dish with Cover" held 1.5 quarts. The partition allowed two items to be prepared and/or served using one casserole at a retail price of $2.95. Lids were interchangeable with other oval casseroles, making either the plain or divided lid usable.

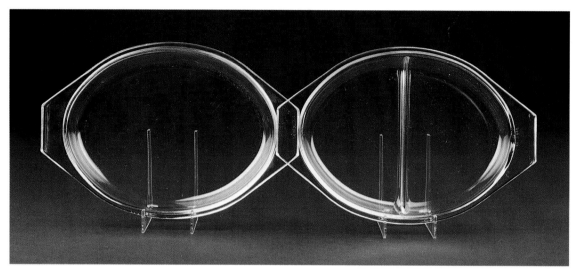

Plain lid and divided lid for the "Cinderella Oval Divided Serving Dish with Cover." $5-7 each.

Delphite is very popular with collectors of kitchen glass. The Delphite divided dish is of great interest to many who are not necessarily PYREX® collectors.

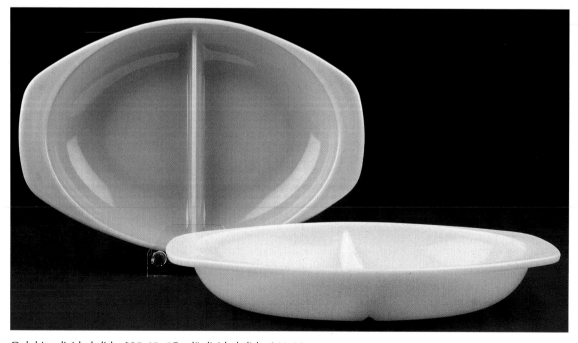

Delphite divided dish, $35-45. "Opal" divided dish, $10-12.

Five different blues illustrate the rainbow of possibilities offered to the consumer. $15-18 each, add $5-7 if a lid is included.

The first divided dishes were offered in 1957 and had white snowflakes on turquoise or charcoal, turquoise snowflakes on white, and white daisies on pink. As acceptance of divided dishes grew, so did the exterior designs and color combinations. Shown is but a sample of the possibilities.

Three divided dishes. The design on the center dish was available in 1958. $20-25 each.

$6.95 bought four "drinkups" and a matching carafe. Drinkups, $5-7 each; carafe, $15-20. Add $5 for the box.

DRINKUPS

The versatility of PYREX® glass is evident in "drinkups," eight ounce beverage mugs. These were available with plastic sleeves in colors that coordinated with other PYREX® colored kitchenware. Drinkups were capable of handling hot or cold drinks.

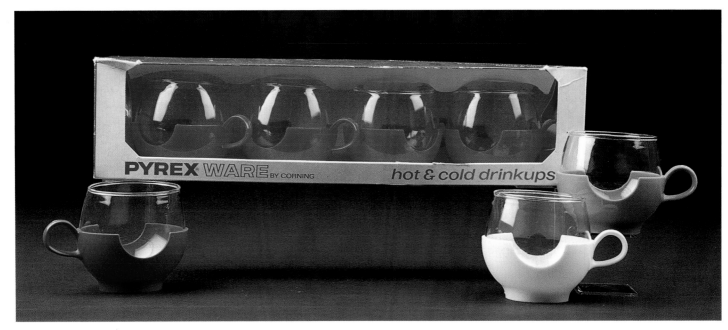

"Drinkups" in an original package and three other colors. $5-7 each. Add $5 for the box.

FIRED-ON GLASSWARE

The interest in these pieces is in the fact that they are fired-on in a jade-ite color. Jade-ite glassware has become one of the most collected categories of kitchen glass. These items are not only uncommon, but blend well with jade-ite collections.

A British-made PYREX® 7.5" long gravy boat and 8" x 4.25" under plate. $100-110.

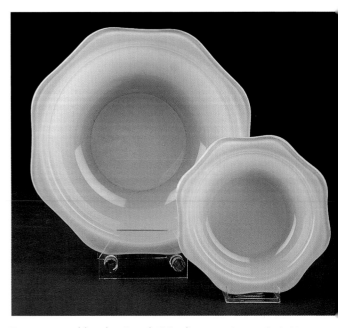

Two octagonal bowls, 9" and 6" in diameter. Large: $50-60; small: $35-40.

LOAF DISHES

Loaf dishes have a 1.5 quart capacity and are most common in solid colors or in Desert Dawn. They have handles that enable the user to grip them easily.

The "Opal" loaf pan measures 10.25" x 5" x 3.5" but is marked: "9 x 5 x 3". The others measure 10" x 5" x 3". $15-20 each.

Four loaf pans. $15-20 each.

PIE PLATES

Although pie plates are marked "8 1/2 INCH" on the bottom, they measure 9.5" across. These "Shallow Baking & Serving Dishes" are found predominately in Lime and Flamingo.

Two pie plates. $10-15 each.

PITCHERS

Pitchers were made in a variety of sizes and shapes, but were specifically intended to hold cool as opposed to hot liquids. Some pitchers were printed with designs that matched other colored PYREX® kitchenware, other pitchers had their own unique embellishments, and a number were plain.

Left: this 7.25" pitcher is marked: "PYREX® USA DO NOT USE ON TOP OF RANGE"; *middle*: a 9" pitcher with a key motif has increments to 60 ounces and is marked: "PYREX® MADE IN USA"; *right*: the original paper sleeve is still in an 8" pitcher with the same mark as the pitcher in the middle. $12-18 each.

"Rings" Beverage Set which is part of Corning Beverage Ware. This set includes one 80 oz. pitcher and 6 twelve oz. tumblers. As shown in box, $65-75.
Courtesy of Janice Johnston/Behind the Green Door

REFRIGERATOR SETS

Marketed as "Oven-Refrigerator Sets" to capitalize on their tolerance of extreme temperatures, these groupings are now commonly referred to simply as refrigerator sets. Along with the 400 bowls, these are among the most desired colored PYREX® kitchen glass items of all. Many collectors remember having refrigerator sets in either their own homes or those of relatives, and are touched with a sense of nostalgia when seeing these sets for sale. Add the characteristics of being attractive, usable, and stackable (to occupy very little space) and refrigerator sets become sought-after by many.

Refrigerator Sets were first made available in 1949 for $3.25. The original set mimicked three of the four colors of the first 400 bowls: yellow, red, and blue. The yellow container was 1.5 quarts, the blue container held 1.5 pints, and the two red containers each were 1.5 cups. The earliest lids are recognizable as having finer ribs. Dirt tends to build up in these ridges. Spray-on oven cleaners are highly effective at cleaning this debris.

$3.25 would purchase the original "PYREX® Ware Oven-and-Refrigerator Set."

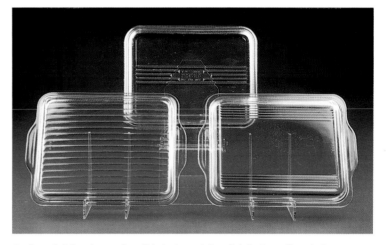

Back and right: the earliest lid designs; *left*: a lid design offered after 1950.

Set 500, an original Oven-Refrigerator Set, with an original label and box. Yellow: $18-20; blue: $15-18; red: $10-12 each. Add $20 for the original labels and $65 for the box.

Clear refrigerator pieces were offered from 1950-1952. They are rarely seen for sale, and few collectors show interest in these pieces. Most are drawn to the colors that seem to say "PYREX®!"

Pink and turquoise refrigerator sets followed. Soon many colors and embellishments were manufactured to match other PYREX® lines. As with other PYREX® colored glassware the original colors, pink and turquoise tend to be the most popular today. Delphite is of interest to collectors of kitchen glass in general, so enjoys a wide appeal. Green, gold, orange, and brown are in less demand.

Two "Opal" and two clear refrigerator dishes. $15-20 each.

Turquoise refrigerator dishes. $15-20 per piece.

Pink refrigerator dishes. $18-25 per piece.

Left: Flowers decorate a refrigerator set in the "Spring Blossom Green" motif that has additional matching pieces including bowls and casseroles; *right*: the "Verde" set. $8-10 per piece.

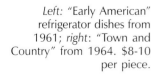

The "Verde" line included refrigerator dishes.

1960s colors on a variety of refrigerator dishes. $8-10 per piece.

Left: "Early American" refrigerator dishes from 1961; *right*: "Town and Country" from 1964. $8-10 per piece.

1960s colors on a variety of refrigerator dishes. Left, "Friendship". $8-10 per piece.

Delphite refrigerator dishes. The Delphite lid on the right is quite unusual. *Left to right:* $40-50, $30-35, $60-70.

Although "Desert Dawn" was only made in pink and yellow, this set of "Homestead" has a similar speckled look. $8-10 per piece.

SALAD SETS

"Coordinated to meet your preparation and serving needs" says it all! This salad set comes complete with the serving bowl, salad fork and spoon, salt and pepper shakers, and vinegar and oil cruets.

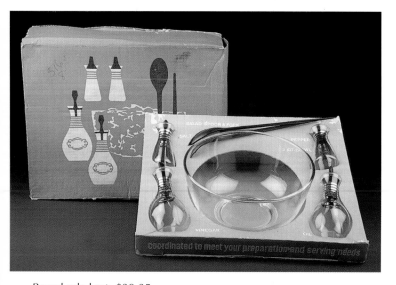

Boxed salad set. $30-35.

"For gracious dining" and $1.95, one could have just the oil and vinegar cruet set. $10-12 per set.

SHAKERS

Salt and pepper shakers in a variety of sizes and shapes were created. Some sets matched other PYREX® glassware, while others simply coordinated with bowls, casseroles, and dinnerware.

Left to right: 5" unmarked shakers with plastic lids, $8-10 per pair; 4.75" shakers with pink plastic lids marked: "PYREX® 2 MADE IN USA," $10-12 per pair; 4" shakers with plastic wood grained lids marked: "PYREX® MADE IN USA NOT FOR FREEZER OR RANGE TOP", $8-10 per pair; 3" shakers with beads, $10-12 per pair.

5" one cup coffee cruet, $10-12; 5.5" salad dressing bottle marked: "PYREX® BRAND GLASSWARE MADE IN USA FOR WEICO," $12-18; salt and pepper shakers, $10-12 per pair.

The small shakers with beaded decorations actually matched a one-cup carafe and a salad dressing bottle. The plastic wrap around the necks of the carafe, bottle, and shakers not only created an interesting decoration but a practical way to easily grip each item.

Corelle livingware also had matching salt and pepper shakers. These unmarked items are 4.5" tall with plastic lids. Corelle patterns, also matching PYREX® kitchen glass, are of interest to some collectors.

Four sets of Corelle livingware shakers. $8-10 per pair.

UTILITY DISHES

Lime and Flamingo oblong utility dishes were first offered in 1952. At $1.35 apiece, these were one of the most expensive bakeware items at the time. Within a few years, additional sizes and colors of these uncovered dishes were made available. However, by the end of the 1950s, bakeware being offered usually included a PYREX® lid, and colorful utility dishes were no long available by the 1960s.

The capacity is not marked on the blue utility dish which measures 10.5" x 7.5" x 2". The "Opal" dish measures 11" x 6.75" x 2.5" and is marked 2 quarts. The lime dish measures 11.5" x 6.5" x 2" and is 1.5 quarts. $15-18 each.

A Flamingo 2 quart utility dish measuring 13" x 8" x 2". $15 -18.

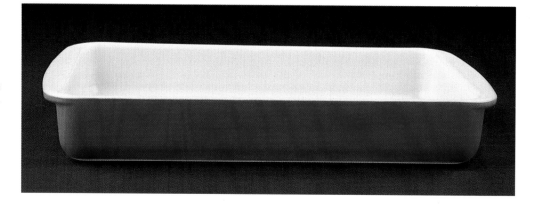

A FINAL LOOK
AT PYREX® COLORS

Tastes change. A simple statement but the key to the success of PYREX® colors. Every effort was made by Corning Glass to supply homemakers with products that met their cooking, baking, serving, and storing needs while complimenting their homes in a colorful way. Practical, durable, and attractive, PYREX® was constantly evolving. If the dimensions of the pieces themselves didn't necessarily change within a given year, one can be certain that the exterior look did undergo some kind of transformation.

Most Americans grew up with some PYREX® colored glassware in their homes. These memories trigger easy recognition which has contributed to its collectibility today.

CHAPTER FOUR

PYREX® TECHNICAL GLASSWARE

The scientists at Corning Glass Works were able to achieve two very important accomplishments. First, they developed low-expansion glass. Simply put, this glassware (which was used in the PYREX® Brand) was capable of tolerating both sudden changes in temperature and extreme temperatures—not only without breaking, but while having minimal changes in size through expansion or contraction. Second, they formulated a glassware that had maximum resistance to deterioration. Chemicals and corrosion had virtually no effect on this glassware, allowing other scientists and researchers the freedom to conduct their work knowing the integrity of their outcomes would not be jeopardized by chemicals leaking from the glass, combining with those being placed inside the glass. There were further ground-breaking discoveries and achievements from the Corning Glass Works scientists, but for the presentation in this chapter, these are the factors that most effect what is pictured.

Collectors of any given subject often have a tendency to expand their focus. PYREX® collectors usually have several pieces of technical glass in their possession. Individuals decorating in a minimalist style are also attracted to PYREX® technical glass. Beakers and flasks make great vases and serving pieces, and funnels certainly have practical applications in the kitchen.

This chapter is designed to provide an overview of some popular PYREX® technical glassware. Think creatively! Most any of these pieces could be used in an interesting and imaginative way in one's home.

BEAKERS

Beakers are available in a huge variety of sizes. A spout allows them to easily adapt to serving salad dressings or cream for coffee. Pictured is but a small representation of the size and style possibilities. Expect to pay anywhere from $1-15 dollars per beaker. The larger the item, the higher the price.

Six beakers from 30 mL through 240 mL.

Six beakers.

BOTTLES

Serving any beverage in a larger-sized bottle would be a fun, attractive alternative to a pitcher. Smaller bottles make adorable bud vases and candleholders. Again, only one's own imagination limits the possibilities.

There are several distinct bottle designs that were created for laboratory uses. A sampling is provided.

3", 7.25", and 14.5" bottles. Prices will run from $1-20 depending on the size of the bottle.

Patented 5-27-19, these two bottles with wicker trim would look wonderful in a domestic environment. $15-20 each.

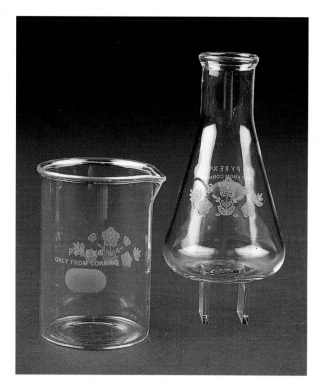

A matching 3.25" beaker and 4.5" bottle marked: "PYREX® ONLY FROM CORNING." $8-12 each.

Eight bottles from 250 mL through 500 mL.

FUNNELS

A PYREX® funnel could certainly be used for its original intent, but consider putting a silk or dried flower in one. Long, narrow tapers would look elegant with a funnel as the base.

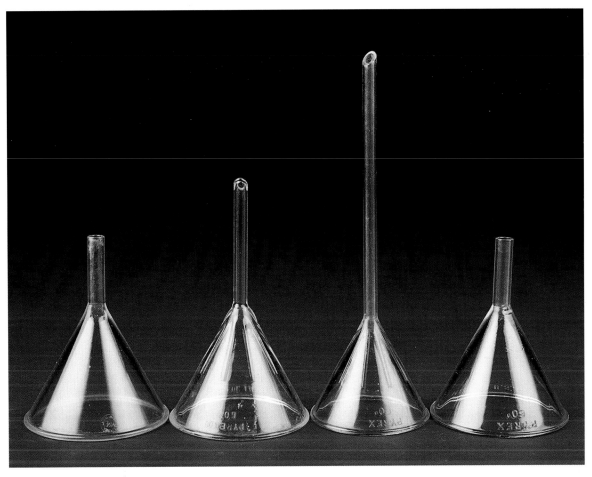

Four funnels. $10-15 each.

A FINAL LOOK AT PYREX®
TECHNICAL GLASS

If not for the stretching of creative minds, PYREX® glassware would not exist. Allow yourself the same freedom of thought; surround your environment with objects that delight and give pleasure. Perhaps a piece of technical glass utilized in an entirely new capacity will bring a small measure of joy to your world.

CHAPTER FIVE

PATTERN
IDENTIFICATION

KNOWN PATTERN NAMES

With the growing popularity of vintage PYREX® collectors are interested in more than owning a nest of bowls like Mother's or a using a few refrigerator dishes to add a colorful touch. I have not been able to determine the names of all of the patterns, but enough are now known to create this identification guide. If you are able to document any of the unknown designs, please contact me using the information inside the front cover of your book.

Autumn Harvest, found in several rust tones.

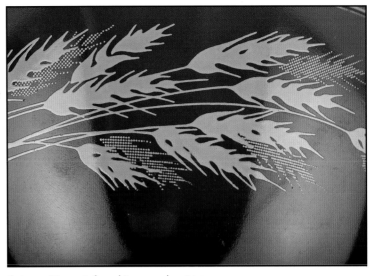

Autumn Harvest, found in several rust tones.

Balloon, used for Chip & Dip set.

Bluebird, used for 1.5 quart casserole.

Brittany Blue.

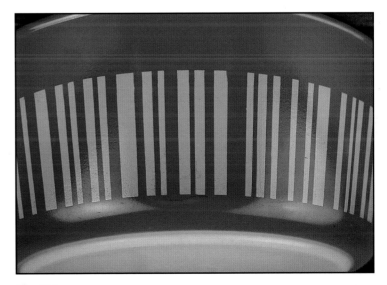

Blue Stripe.

Bride's Casserole.

Butterfly Gold, found in several shades and variations.

Butterfly Gold, found in several shades and variations.

Butterfly Gold, found in several shades and variations.

Butterfly Gold, found in several shades and variations.

Butterprint, found in yellow, turquoise, and pink. Variations include one of the three colors on white and white on one of these three colors.

Butterprint, found in turquoise, yellow, and pink. Variations include one of the three colors on white and white on one of these three colors.

Butterprint, found in turquoise, yellow, and pink. Variations include one of the three colors on white and white on one of these three colors.

Butterprint, found in turquoise, yellow, and pink. Variations include one of the three colors on white and white on one of these three colors.

Crazy Daisy, also made with green on white.

Colonial Mist.

Colonial Mist.

Daisy. This yellow and orange version was used in bowls, refrigerator pieces, and more.

Daisy. This pink and white version was used on casseroles briefly in the 1950s.

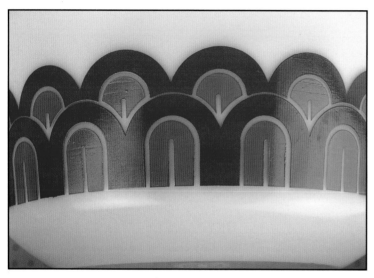

Designs, found in gold arches with orange and orange arches with gold.

Early American, found in brown and white, white and brown, and with gold.

Early American, found in brown and white, white and brown, and with gold.

Early American, found in brown and white, white and brown, and with gold.

Early American, found in brown and white, white and brown, and with gold.

Early American, found in brown and white, white and brown, and with gold.

Forest Fancies.

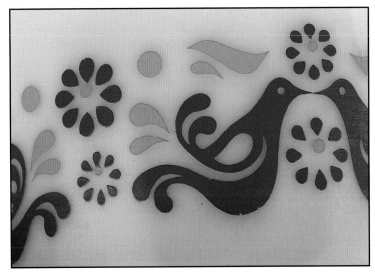

Friendship.

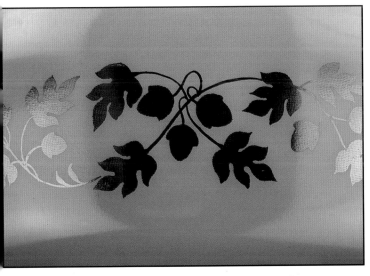

Golden Acorn.

Golden Honeysuckle.

Gooseberry, found in white on pink, pink on white, black on yellow, and black on white.

Gooseberry, found in pink on white, white on pink, black on yellow, and black on white.

Gooseberry, found in black on white, black on yellow, pink on white, and white on pink.

Homestead. Some pieces have speckles and no blue design.

Horizon.

Horizon Blue.

Medallion.

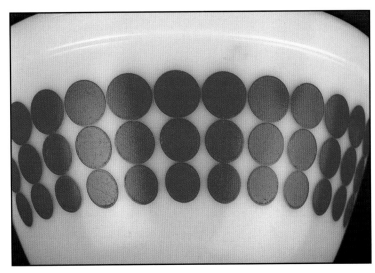

New Dot. Not pictured is the avocado green dots found on the 404 bowl.

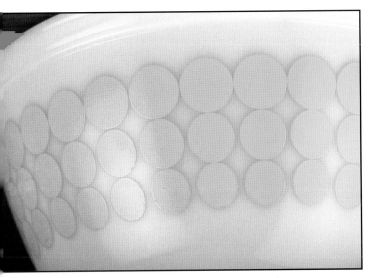

New Dot. Not pictured is the avocado green dots found on the 404 bowl.

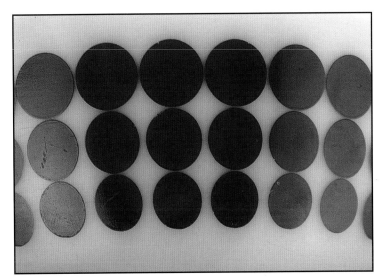

New Dot. Not pictured is the avocado green dots found on the 404 bowl.

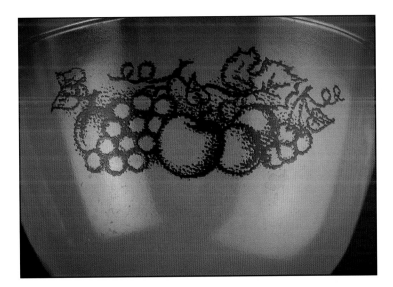

Old Orchard, found in several shades of brown.

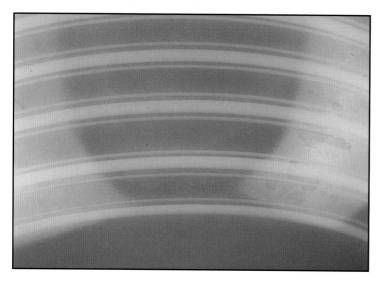

Rainbow Stripes. Not pictured is pink stripes.

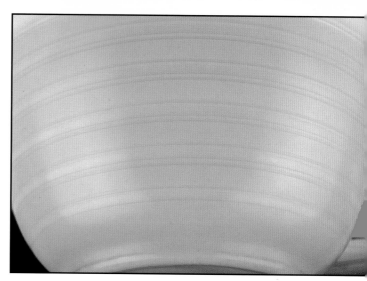

Rainbow Stripes. Not pictured is pink stripes.

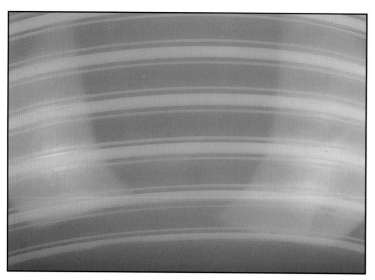

Rainbow Stripes. Not pictured is pink stripes.

Sandalwood, found in tan on white and white on tan.

Snowflake, found in two arrangement: larger snowflakes in a straight line and smaller snowflakes in two rows. Colors include white on turquoise, turquoise on white, and white on charcoal.

Snowflake, found in two arrangement: larger snowflakes in a straight line and smaller snowflakes in two rows. Colors include white on turquoise, turquoise on white, and white on charcoal.

Snowflake, found in two arrangement: larger snowflakes in a straight line and smaller snowflakes in two rows. Colors include white on turquoise, turquoise on white, and white on charcoal.

Snowflake, found in two arrangement: larger snowflakes in a straight line and smaller snowflakes in two rows. Colors include white on charcoal, white on turquoise, and turquoise on white.

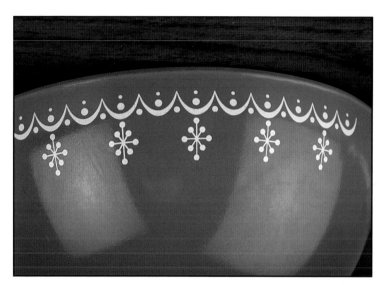

Snowflake, found in two arrangement: larger snowflakes in a straight line and smaller snowflakes in two rows. Colors include white on charcoal, white on turquoise, and turquoise on white.

Snowflake Blue, found in white on blue and blue on white.

Snowflake Blue, found in blue on white and white on blue.

Spring Blossom Green, found in white on green and green on white.

Spring Blossom Green, found in green on white and white on green.

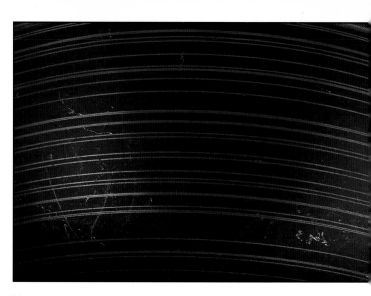

Terra.

Town and Country, found in several color combinations.

Town and Country, found in several color combinations.

Town and Country, found in several color combinations.

Tulip.

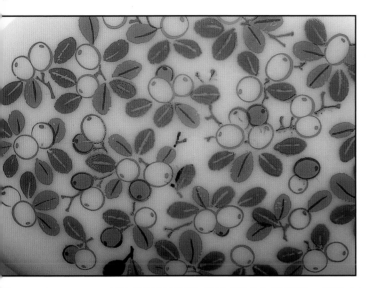

Verde. This motif is found on lids. Bases and bowls are solid colored.

Woodland, found in shades of brown.

Woodland, found in shades of brown.

Found on a casserole.

THE UNKNOWNS

Found on a casserole.

Found on a casserole.

Found on a divided dish.

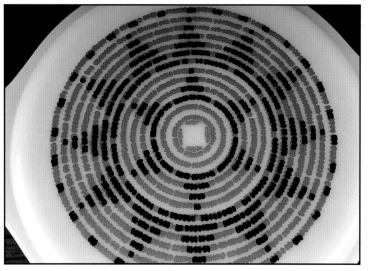

Found on a lid.

Found on a lid.

Found on a lid. The base of this casserole rests in a plastic cradle.

Found on a lid.

Found on Lid.

Found on mugs, creamers, and sugar bowls.

Found on mugs, creamers, and sugar bowls.

Found on mugs, creamers, and sugar bowls.

Found on a casserole.

Found on a casserole.

Found on a casserole.

Found on a casserole.

Found on a divided dish.

Found on a casserole, this is similar to Horizon Blue pictured earlier and Golden Scroll pictured on page 113.

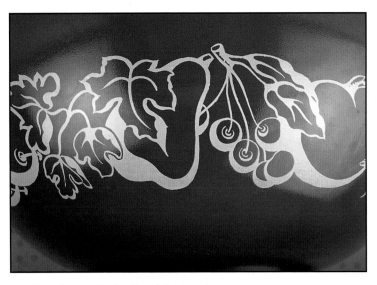

Found on a Cinderella mixing bowl.

Found on a Cinderella mixing bowl.

Found on a variety of pieces in one band as shown or with two bands.

Found on a 404 mixing bowl.